15 00

HEALING BREATH

D0711101

ECOLOGY AND JUSTICE
An Orbis Series on Global Ecology

The Orbis Series *Ecology and Justice* publishes books that religiously and theologically integrate concerns for our imperilled Earth as an interconnected life system with concerns for just and sustainable social and economic systems that benefit the entire human community.

Books in the Series seek ways to:
- free human beings, animals, and the Earth as-a-whole from exploitative bondage
- understand and develop visions of life on Earth that increase sensitivity to ecological issues in an integrative manner
- deepen appreciation and expand dialogue on the theological and spiritual ramifications of the cosmological depths of the heart of life
- promote inclusive, participative strategies that enhance the struggle of the Earth's voiceless poor for justice.

Viewing the present moment as a challenge to responsible creativity, the Series seeks authors who speak to ecojustice concerns and who bring into dialogue and debate a range of Christian, secular, world religions, scientific, and new paradigms of thought.

Also in the Series

John B. Cobb, Jr., *Sustainability: Economics, Ecology, and Justice*
Charles Pinches and Jay B. McDaniel, editors, *Good News for Animals?*
Frederick Ferré, *Hellfire & Lightning Rods*

ECOLOGY AND JUSTICE SERIES

HEALING BREATH

Zen Spirituality for a Wounded Earth

Ruben L. F. Habito

ORBIS BOOKS

Maryknoll, New York 10545

The Catholic Foreign Mission Society of America (Maryknoll) recruits and trains people for overseas missionary service. Through Orbis Books, Maryknoll aims to foster the international dialogue that is essential to mission. The books published, however, reflect the opinions of their authors and are not meant to represent the official position of the society.

Copyright © 1993 by Ruben L. F. Habito
All rights reserved
Manufactured in the United States of America

Library of Congress Cataloging in Publication Data

Habito, Ruben L. F., 1947-
    Healing breath : Zen spirituality for a wounded earth / Ruben L. F. Habito.
        p.   cm. — (Ecology and justice series)
    Includes bibliographical references and index.
    ISBN 0-88344-919-6 (pbk.)
    1. Spiritual life—Zen Buddhism.   2. Zen Buddhism—Doctrines. I. Title.   II. Series: Ecology and justice.
BQ9288.H33   1993
294.3'444—dc20   93-5125
                                                                        CIP

Printed on recycled paper

To
Yamada Koun Roshi (1907-1989)
and
Fr. Hugo Enomiya-Lassalle, S.J. (1898-1990)
in boundless gratitude

Contents

Acknowledgments

This book comes out of reflections based on many years of assisting at and directing Zen retreats (*sesshin**) in Asia, Europe, and the United States. I am grateful to so many individuals whom I have been privileged to meet in all these retreats, who have sat with me, who have posed challenging questions, who have taught me so many valuable things in life.

Much of what is written in this book has also been inspired through encounters with many persons in grassroots communities in Asian countries, including my own country, the Philippines, India, Indonesia, Thailand, and Hong Kong, as well as Japan, where I lived for nearly two decades. In these encounters I came to realize the need for all of us to keep touching base with the pulse of those bearing the brunt of the unjust and destructive structures in our world, and with those continually risking their lives as they engage themselves in tasks toward the transformation of such structures.

It has been in those precious times spent with grassroots communities in different places that I have come face-to-face with the woundedness that we all bear as members of this Earth community. During those visits to these communities, I have been privileged to experience in various ways the power of cosmic compassion at work toward the healing of a wounded Earth. To all those persons whom I encountered in these grassroots communities, living and dead, I continue to bow my head in profoundest gratitude.

The late Yamada Koun Roshi, my master in the dharma, and the late Fr. Hugo Enomiya-Lassalle, S.J., my Jesuit spiritual director, are two pillars who have formed the spiritual foundations of what I am, and to these two I dedicate this book.

Countless friends and benefactors have led me by the hand

and helped me reach out to other fellow beings. Among these, I thank especially Sr. Elaine MacInnes, OLM, also a disciple of Yamada Roshi. She is the founder of several Zen centers in the Philippines and has been of tremendous support through the years. A person I cannot thank enough is Sr. Mary Rosario Battung, RGS, who continues to be an inspiration from afar, as an embodiment of a true Zen person, a "hearer of the sounds of the world." Sr. Vicky Palanca, ICM, has also been supportive through the years.

I am deeply grateful to Robert Aitken Roshi, known to many as the Dean of American Zen, an elder brother in the dharma whom I deeply respect and admire, for his encouragement, especially in the crucial period of my life transition. Likewise to Fr. Heinrich Dumoulin, S.J., Fr. Michael Amaladoss, S.J., and Fr. Adolfo Nicolas, S.J., whose guidance and continued friendship have meant so much.

The Center for Action and Contemplation, headed by Fr. Richard Rohr, OFM, based in Albuquerque, New Mexico, has given me the opportunity, through its annually sponsored Encounters of the Heart retreats, of sharing with small groups what later emerged as the kernel of this book. Heartfelt gratitude goes especially to Christina Spahn, its Co-Director, and all of those associated with this Center, from whom I have learned and received so much.

I also would like to express thanks to friends, mentors, and advisers who took time to read the manuscript and give very valuable suggestions for its improvement through several revisions: Jay McDaniel, Paul Knitter, Donald Mitchell, Thomas Green, S.J., Ana Maria Schluter, Susan Jion Postal, Thelma Hall, R.C , Pascaline Coff, OSB, Frances Meenan, Paula Cooey, Roy Hamric, John Ockels, William McElvaney, Bill Eakin, and Florian Reis. Special thanks to Bill Burrows, Robert Ellsberg, and the Orbis staff, for their help and valuable suggestions.

Untold gratitude to my parents, brothers, and sisters and their families, who have been a constant support through the ups and downs of life; to Maria Dorothea, my beloved wife, partner, constructive critic, and companion in this journey that has taken some surprising turns. May I also express my heartfelt hopes for our two sons, Florian Estanislao and Benjamin Norbert, that they may go on in life grateful for the gifts of Earth. As they bear their share of its wounds, may they also take an active part in its healing.

Glossary of Zen Terms

Bodhisattva: Literally, a "being-toward-enlightment," one who is set on the path of awakening and who lives in selfless devotion for the liberation of all sentient beings.

dokusan: One-to-one interview with the Zen teacher. Literally, "to go alone." Also called *sanzen* ("to go to Zen interview").

Heart Sutra: A short Buddhist scriptural text summarizing the nature and extolling the virtues of enlightenment. It is also an excellent, rhythmical liturgical text used for chanting in Zen halls.

kensho: The experience of awakening to one's true self. Literally, "seeing (one's own true) nature."

kinhin: Walking Zen. In formal Zen practice, periods of seated meditation *(zazen)* are interspersed by short intervals of walking in a formal and methodical way.

koan: An anecdote or question given by the Zen teacher to the practitioner in a one-to-one interview as a help in deepening the latter's practice. This usually involves a problematic situation or riddle that cannot be solved by the discursive or logical mind and invites the practitioner to a direct experience leading to Zen awakening.

This glossary lists words having asterisks on their first appearance in the text.

Rinzai: One of the Zen sects (or schools) transplanted from China that took root and flowered in Japan. Founded by Lin-chi I-hsuan (Japanese, Rinzai Gigen) (d. 866), it is characterized by an aggressive and militant approach to practice, employing shouts and slaps to jolt the practitioner and provide external impetus for the experience of awakening. This school is known also for the development of koan practice as a help to the same.

Roshi: The formal title of one who has received transmission in a Zen lineage and is authorized to hand down this lineage to others. Literally, "old teacher."

San-un Zendo: The Zen Hall of the Three Clouds, a small Zen hall located in Kamakura, Japan, established by Yamada Koun Roshi (1907-1989), which has become an internationally known center of practice.

sesshin: A Zen retreat, usually lasting from five to eight days or longer. Literally, "encounter of the heart."

shikan taza: Single-minded sitting. In this way of practice, one simply sits in full awareness of every present moment. Literally, "just sitting through and through."

Soto: A school (or sect) of Zen practice begun in China, named after two of its prominent ancestors, Ts'ao-shan Pen-chi (Japanese, *So*zan Honjaku) (840-901) and Tung-shan Liang-chieh (Japanese: *To*zan Ryokai) (807-869). Zen master Dogen (1200-1253) received transmission in this lineage during a short sojourn in China and transmitted it on in Japan. Its practice is characterized by emphasis on stillness and perfect transparency in seated meditation, as well as the accent on living one's daily life as the embodiment of enlightenment.

teisho: An exhortatory talk given by an authorized Zen
              teacher to spur listeners in their practice and
              lead to the experience of awakening.

zazen: Seated Zen meditation.

Introduction

This book presents Zen as a spirituality and way of life that can lead to healing in the personal, social, and ecological dimensions of our being.

First, it is written for those in search of ways of deepening their personal spirituality. They may be individuals who have come to an awareness of their own brokenness and woundedness, who see the fragmentation and disorientation, the vacuity in their lives. Such persons may, in all this, also hear a voice from within, urging them to a search for wholeness or a sense of groundedness and connectedness. This book offers practical steps that can be taken in following that inner voice, with a map of the terrain that awaits to be explored and an account of some of the things in store for those who follow the path.

Second, it is for those who are sensitive to what is happening in the world around us and have come to be acutely aware of the woundedness of the Earth community as a whole. They are those who share the perception that we on this planet are in a critical state and are heading for disaster, if we don't shape up and radically change our ways. Many of us may already be engaged in some form of social or ecological action as our way of responding to the situation from different contexts. We may have already experienced how active involvement in socio-ecological tasks can open us to a new level of spiritual awareness, and thus have come to be concerned with nurturing such a spirituality that would continue to empower us and affirm us in this kind of engagement.

On the other hand, we may have been overwhelmed by the magnitude of the task before us. We may have been tempted to pessimism or raised our hands in despair, noting that our best efforts, while perhaps able to stem the damage to some extent,

1

are not able to make any significant change in the overall picture. This book is addressed to such persons as a testament of hope and an invitation to a renewed vision of global healing.

This book does not propose any new course of action, any new strategy for our social and ecological recovery or well-being. What it does offer is a description of and an invitation to practice that can open one to a *way of seeing* that leads to right living and right action toward healing our ailing Earth community.

Father Thomas Berry, a prophet of our generation who has called attention to Earth's woundedness and to the urgent need for us to take this situation more seriously, points out that our basic problem, more than one of strategy, is one of *cosmology*.[1] Our current situation is based on a misguided and mistaken view of the cosmos, which in turn begets attitudes that result in destructive and violent behavior toward one another and toward Earth. By being able to perceive our socio-ecological malaise as fundamentally rooted in an erroneous view of things, we are able to see that our healing depends on our coming to a *right view* of the way things are.[2] This book presents a step-by-step process that we can begin right from where we are, from our concrete situation in daily life, that can lead us to that right view.

Unfortunately, personal spirituality and engagement in socio-ecological tasks tend to be regarded as different things altogether. We see all too often that those pursuing the one have not necessarily occupied themselves with the other. There is, however, a growing number among us who realize the vital connection, and thus the need for the integration of these two concerns. This book presents a way that can ground such an integration. Our personal woundedness is not unrelated to the woundedness of Earth as a whole. Consequently, our healing as Earth community cannot be separate from our healing as individual persons who make up that community, and vice versa.

There is a third kind of person I hope to address in these pages, one who may also identify with either or both of the kinds of persons described above. I refer to those persons, including many whom I have met in the course of assisting in Zen retreats in different places over the past decade, who find their spiritual roots in the Christian tradition and are raising questions about this tradition from different angles. I have sensed a certain kind of woundedness in many of these persons. It may be from carrying a considerable amount of baggage imposed upon them by particular forms of Western Christianity. It may be a lingering sense of guilt, a sense of disillusionment, or a sense of betrayal from different kinds of experiences associated with their religious upbringing. It may be the rootless feeling due to one's separation from the religion of one's early childhood, one which may have given a sense of belonging and security at a certain stage of one's life, but whose geographical, social, or theological boundaries are now too narrow for one to continue to remain inside those boundaries.

Many persons with this background have abandoned their childhood faith altogether. Others continue to identify themselves as Christian, while standing in critical distance from any particular church congregation, for different kinds of reasons. There are also others who continue to go to church and receive the sacraments, yet are led to explore ways of deepening their spirituality in forms other than what institutional church life can offer. What these persons have in common is a continuing search for a deeper and more meaningful participation in the spiritual dimension than either their early religious formation gave them a taste of, or the struggles of their later life have opened them to. In this book we attempt to address some of the basic issues involved in such a search, especially keeping in mind those for whom Christian symbols and biblical themes may find sympathetic resonance.

Over the years of assisting at Zen retreats, I have been asked questions such as: Can a Christian practice genuine Zen? Is Zen practice compatible with a Christian faith commitment? What kind of belief system does Zen presuppose or require for one to fully engage in it? What effect does spiritual practice in an Eastern religious tradition have on Christian life and understanding? I have been challenged and helped by such questions, and have been inspired to write this book in the hope of being able to present a response to some of these questions.[3]

In the course of my Zen journey over the years, I myself have had to struggle and come to grips with the Christian faith in which I was born and raised. It would need another book to unpack all this, but to make a long story short, Zen practice has invited me to listen with renewed fervor and attention to the Good News brought by Jesus, proclaiming the reign of God in our midst. If anything, Zen practice has enabled me to appreciate and reaffirm the dynamism and the possibilities of the Christian Gospel message, while at the same time becoming more critical of the ways in which many of us who profess adherence to it have sanitized, distorted, muffled, or institutionalized it, or have used it for our own egoistic purposes, whether consciously or unconsciously.

What I present here is a personal testimony coming out of an experience of *intrareligious dialogue.* This is a term that refers to an encounter of two religious traditions within the same individual.[4] In this kind of religious encounter, the same individual is invited to place herself *within* the differing religious traditions being considered, and let these traditions meet and discover mutual resonances and throw light upon one another, as well as mutually challenge one another from the perspective of the core message of each.

More and more of our contemporaries are beginning to engage and find fruit in intrareligious encounters of this kind, as we open our eyes and simply recognize the prevailing presence and the dynamic power of the living religious traditions coexisting in our global village.[5]

Our global situation calls for attention from all of us as members of this Earth community, from whatever religious tradition we come, or whether we profess religious affiliation or not. This book will outline the key elements of Zen as a way of practice and spirituality which, though historically coming from the Buddhist tradition, cuts across traditional religious boundaries[6] and leads to a new way of seeing, and likewise grounds an active engagement in tasks addressing our critical situation. By no means do we imply that Zen is the only way or even a preferred way over other spiritual paths in this regard.[7] It is presented here as a spirituality of engagement suited for a postmodern world, as one concrete way to a transformed consciousness that can ground us in our quest for personal and global healing.[8]

1.

Toward Healing

Tracing the Roots of Our Woundedness

Recognizing an ailing situation exists is a crucial step toward its healing. Conversely, genuine healing can be hampered by a state of mind that refuses to recognize there is a problem.[1] However, as we open our eyes to what is happening in the world around us, it becomes more difficult to maintain such an attitude of denial.

In this chapter we will begin with a broad survey of the manifestations of our ailing condition as Earth community and as individuals making up that community. We will then attempt to trace the root cause of this situation, in a stance that regards nature, our fellow human beings, and our very own selves, as Other. With this in the background, we will present a very rough outline of Buddhist and Christian ways of diagnosing the human condition. This will set the stage for the following chapters, wherein we consider key aspects of Zen practice and spirituality as a way of addressing our situation.

MANIFESTATIONS OF OUR WOUNDEDNESS

Many things around us tell us that all is not well. Let us take a quick scan of our situation on the ecological, social, and personal levels of our existence, for a general picture of the task before us.

First, on a global ecological angle, the woundedness of Earth is brought to our attention from all quarters. Acid rain, toxic wastes, radioactive contamination, depleting ozone layer, denudation of forests, desertification, and extinction of species, among others, are now phrases that have become part of our everyday vocabulary. The situation comes home to us as we feel the effects in the food we eat, the water we drink, the air we breathe. This is already taking its toll on the next generation, with an increasing number of infants being born with different kinds of abnormalities and obstacles to a normal life, thought to be linked with the proliferation of toxic material in the very matrix that nurtures our life itself, Earth.[2]

Second, our malaise on this global ecological level is not unrelated to the deep wounds of our contemporary human society. By this we mean the network and structures of our interhuman relations, not only as individuals with one another, but insofar as we belong to different groupings, based on race, economic class, ideology, religious affiliation, nationality, and so on.

On this level, many forms of violence between humans continue to be perpetrated, only a fraction of these reaching the media or the criminal courts. Right at this moment, armed conflicts are going on in different parts of the world, for various ethnic, ideological, economic, and other reasons, with their toll in human lives. Even in the family, where life is supposed to be nurtured instead of threatened or harmed, violence is an everyday reality that gnaws at the very core of our human nature and puts us at a loss as to where we should place our trust in life.

Besides the actual physical violence that humans perpetrate against one another in different forms, there is violence that we can call structural. This is the kind that continues in a systemic way to take its toll in so many lives, as well as diminishing the quality of life on Earth.[3] For example, according to recent reports, approximately 60,000 children die daily of hunger-related causes throughout the world. Many of those children may not be victims of direct physical violence, but they are deprived of their right to life by not having enough nutrition to sustain it, and are thus victims of a structural kind of violence. This is connected with factors such as poverty, unhygienic conditions in their living surroundings, lack of access to medical facilities, and so on.

In short, a stark look at the concrete human situation in various societies throughout the world today brings to light the many different forms of physical and structural violence that we humans continue to perpetrate upon one another, manifesting our brokenness as human community. These include different forms of violations of basic human rights, discrimination based on race, gender, religion, ethnic background, or other factors.

Third, on the individual, personal level, each of us bears within ourselves wounds inflicted upon us since birth, or even before. These may be wounds inflicted by parents who were not ready for parenting at the time we came into their lives, or who may not have been able to communicate their love to us at the time we most needed it. These may be wounds from a dysfunctional family that failed to give us a sense of security and a sense of being accepted in the world. These may be wounds of betrayal from someone we trusted, someone we looked up to. These may be wounds from someone to whom we gave love and affection but did not receive in return. These may be wounds from a broken relationship, from a human tragedy such as the death of a loved one, or unhealed wounds from an act of violence on our person that continues to haunt our soul.

Also, as I look at myself and examine what motivates me in my behavior, in my goals, in my ambitions, I see I have a false image of myself, which I constantly pursue or carry around with me. Such a false image may be due to some ideal I carry of what I want to be but am not yet. It may be based on an unconscious imposition of expectations placed upon me by my parents, my peers, those I respect and admire, those that I compete with. It may be based on a picture imprinted upon my consciousness or my subconscious by the media which bombards me with images of the "beautiful people" — people I "should" be like, if I am to be a person of worth.

My personal woundedness and brokenness is brought home to me as I see myself going through life in a way that is not really me. This makes itself felt in the lack of peace I find within

myself, in my failure to accept myself for what I am, in my
inability to feel at home wherever I am. All this in turn drives
me to seek some form of diversion that will only aggravate my
brokenness. I may turn to alcohol or drugs, or wanton sexual
activity. I may turn to television, or some other engaging and
time-consuming diversion, or else bury myself in my work. I may
seek solace in an unhealthy relationship with another person,
the kind of relationship called co-dependent, and so on. In short,
the various forms of addiction plaguing so many of us in today's
society can be understood in the light of this need to hold onto
something to cushion us from our inner insecurity at not being
able to live authentic lives.

My own brokenness as an individual leads me to behave in
ways that are destructive toward my fellow humans, life, and the
world in general. We tend to inflict wounds upon one another
as a way of retaliating for the personal wounds that have been
inflicted upon us from all sides. The finding that many convicted
child molesters or sexual abusers have been victims of child or
sexual abuse themselves is an indication of this. Being victims
ourselves, the unhealed wounds in our being drive us to victimize
those around us, beginning with those we love the most.

Taking an objective look at all this, we are able to see the
interconnected nature of the wounds we bear in the ecological,
social, and personal dimensions of our being. All these put
together is what we refer to as the *wounded Earth*. In other
words, *Earth* means not just *the earth*, seen as an object out there,
as opposed to and distinguished from us as its human inhabi-
tants, who presume to have some mode of control over it or
even some mandate to "manage it" (i.e., as its stewards). What
we refer to rather is the interconnected reality that is the matrix
of life itself, including mountains and rivers as well as all sentient
beings, and not excluding us humans, who find ourselves right
at the heart of this reality, as its consciousness.[4] Earth is us, and
we are Earth. To talk of a broken Earth is to talk of our very
brokenness itself, the woundedness of the very fabric of interconnected life that makes us what we are and affects us all as
members of this Earth community.

In this context, the hole in the ozone layer is not just some
perforation in the sky somewhere out there, but a hole that cuts

right through our own being. The toxic wastes we have scattered over land, air, and sea are not just loads of harmful garbage we can and must shield ourselves from with further technological ingenuity, but are poisons already seeping into our very system and threatening the flow of life itself. The violence brought about by ethnic and ideological conflicts in different places of the world is violence inflicted upon us all. Also in this context, the woundedness we humans feel deep within our souls from our broken relationships or from the unfulfilled desires of a craving ego, manifested in our addictions, are as much part of Earth's woundedness as the social and ecological wounds described above. To put it in other terms, we find ourselves, as Earth community, in a *dysfunctional* situation, and are in need of healing on the many different levels of our existence. Healing Earth's wounds, then, is healing our very own selves, on the manifold and interrelated levels this woundedness makes itself felt to us.

TRACING THE ROOTS OF OUR BROKENNESS

The awareness of our woundedness on the global-ecological, social, and personal levels of our existence leads us to ask: what is behind all this? We are invited to look deeper and trace the root causes of our situation of woundedness, in order to see more clearly what steps need to be taken toward our own healing.

Nature as Other

As we examine the fundamental attitude that lies behind our conflict-oriented and violent modes of behavior, we note first of all how we have come to view the natural world as Other, to be tamed and controlled and brought into submission for our human purposes.[5] It is our way of seeing the natural world — that which is actually the very source of our being as well as of our nurture — in opposition to us that has resulted in our destructive attitudes and acts toward it.

With the so-called progress we have made in science and

technology, the natural world is no longer a wild Other that stands against us in a hostile or inimical way, as some earlier societies may have regarded it. We have subjected it to our measuring instruments as an object of inquiry and have come to know much about its secrets and patterns of behavior. Our sophisticated telescopes reach into the far-out galaxies, our spaceships are on the way to the outlying areas of our solar system. We have succeeded in splitting what was once considered to be the indivisible atom, and our electron microscopes continue to probe into the intricacies of subatomic particles. We have even reached down to the genetic zone, and are able to make alterations in the makeup of humans yet to be born. All this has tended to give us the impression that we are now in control.

Our very use of language reveals this attitude of viewing the natural world as Other: it is our *environment* which provides us with resources that we need for the maintenance of our being. We humans, gifted with rationality, see ourselves as at the pinnacle of a hierarchy of being, and everything else around us is regarded as subservient to our purposes and designs. As the disastrous effects of what we have done to the natural world come to impinge upon us, the well-intentioned among us say that we must "protect our environment," we must "conserve our depleting resources."

Such voices, while having done all of us a great service by calling our attention to the urgency and criticality of our situation and leading to a great deal of beneficial action, remain based on the same presupposition that is at the root of our malady: nature is Other to us. The difference in emphasis they do make is that, for our own good, we must treat this Other kindly, so it will be kind to us. But if we continue to maintain that basic attitude of regarding nature as Other to us, we will not be able to address the root cause of our malady.[6] To paraphrase Thomas Berry, improvements in *strategy* will not make up for a fundamental gap in our *cosmology.*

The Gaze of Other People

Our view of the natural world as Other is not unrelated to our way of regarding our fellow humans. Other people impinge

upon my freedom, since I am always subjected to their judgmental gaze or they stand in the way of my desire to do or
possess things I want. Insofar as I regard them as Other, I find
myself in a state of constant conflict and opposition vis-à-vis my
fellow human beings, beginning with my own parents, siblings,
and everyone else I encounter in my journey through life.

Such a stance of "I" versus Other passes on from the individual level to the corporate entity we identify with, whether it
be the neighborhood gang, the ethnic group we belong to, our
economic class, religious body, nation-state, and so on. This
stance is what lies at the root of the violent conflict among
human groupings. Nation-states, ethnic groups, religious bodies,
economic classes, business corporations, or neighborhood gangs
often come to cross-purposes for various reasons, be they ter-
ritorial rights, economic advantage, ideological differences,
religious belief, or simple differences in approach to things. A
situation of conflict can be triggered by differences as trivial as
the way we break an egg (to cite a noted caricature from *Gul-
liver's Travels*).

The physical violence we humans perpetrate upon one
another—from the internecine struggles among tribal communities to violence of the magnitude of the Holocaust and Hiroshima, from police brutality and racially motivated riots to rape,
wife beating and child abuse—all stems from this stance wherein
we regard our fellow human beings as Other.

We see structural violence that has effects of global proportions, where a small percentage of the world's population can
afford to wallow in luxury and wasteful consumption while hun-
dreds of millions live in dehumanizing poverty; where 60,000
children die of hunger-related causes every day while much of
the grain produced by the world goes to cattle; where the rich
get richer and the poor get poorer.

We can analyze all this and present different strategies for
change, based on different ideological positions. But at rock
bottom, there is a basic attitude at the root of all this—the stance
that sets our fellow humans at arm's length, regarding them as
Other than ourselves.

We can go on living our lives in our comfortable corners,
preoccupied with our own affairs, so what happens to others

does not enter our realm of concern—it is their concern, not ours. If we do get some twinge of conscience, enough to send in a check now and then to some organization helping the poor and less privileged of this Earth, we breathe a sigh of thanks that it is not *our* children, and that we ourselves are blessed, not like those unfortunate others whom we may even include in our intercessory prayers.

Needless to say, the different kinds of violence continually being inflicted upon human beings throughout different parts of the world—including denial of the basic right to life and liberty to so many, the acts and attitudes of discrimination based on race, religious belonging, gender, or sexual preference, and so on—likewise stem from the attitude that relegates our fellow humans to the realm of the Other.

Other to My Own Self

The stance that regards our fellow human beings as Other comes from a supposition that there exists something called "I" that is properly myself, in opposition to those others.

It is this supposition, which we carry with us throughout our lives, that determines the way we relate to the natural world and to our fellow humans, and the way we project ourselves in the world. It is this supposition—that I am here and the rest of the world is out there—upon which we base our daily lives. This is a mode of life based on the ego-centered consciousness.

This "I" with which we relate to the world needs to be affirmed in its existence through the recognition of those around it, beginning with the first human beings it comes into contact with, its natural parents. Also, as an embodied being, it needs food, clothing, shelter, and other goods to ensure its nurture and continued existence in this world. Further on, it becomes conscious of other needs and wants, not only for more material goods, but also more manifestations of affection, praise, esteem, approbation. If these are not easy in coming, then it begins to devise ways to obtain them by behaving in certain ways so those around it will notice its existence. Within a few months of birth, an infant tends in this direction, and as it grows in age and wisdom in the ways of the world, the means that will be employed to obtain such needs and wants will also grow in variety and nuance.

In all this, the idea that the "I" is in here, as opposed to the rest of the world out there, is normally taken for granted and not placed into question.

But there have been always a few blessed ones among us who, by some touch of grace, may have been able to see through the veil of separation that we call the ego-centered consciousness. Such individuals, the mystics and saints among us, are able to experience a deeper dimension of reality than what the ordinary consciousness presents, and are able to bridge the seeming opposition between the "I" in here and the world "out there." Such individuals have lived in different historical epochs and in different parts of the world, and they bear witness to the inexhaustible possibilities and the unfathomable grandeur of being. These are persons who, in their very mode of being, serve as pointers to all of us, to a dimension in our very depths wherein lies the healing of our woundedness.[7] This is a dimension that takes us beyond our ordinary way of looking at the world, cutting through the separation between the "I" and the Other that we tend to assume with our ego-consciousness.

As long as our view of things is governed by this ego-centered consciousness, we think of the "I" as a separate entity from the rest of the world. This "I" is quite vulnerable and capable of being wounded, because it will not get what it wants or needs every time in its dealings with human beings and the natural world, since it considers these as separate from itself and in constant opposition and struggle.

The "I" must protect itself by putting on a mask (*persona* in Latin) or by creating an idealized image of itself to carry it through its dealings with those others out there.

In moments of clarity, we can see that the idealized image we have created for ourselves takes over in our dealings with our fellow beings. The "I" that is viewed as separate from the rest of the world tends to put on a mask to protect it and to aid it in dealing with the world.

This is the "I" that wants to meet the expectations of its parents and its peers; that wants to keep up with the Joneses; that wants to wear designer clothes or ride around in classy cars;

that wants to get the attention of the world; that wants to be in control of its own as well as other people's lives. As we pursue such a concocted and idealized image, we stray from the reality that is our true self and thus aggravate our own woundedness.

With this view of the "I" in opposition to the rest of the world, we carry with us throughout our lives a wounded ego whose tendency is, in its own defense, to retaliate and go inflict more wounds upon those it regards as Other—fellow humans and the Earth, no less than upon its own self.

We can thus trace the root cause of our woundedness in this stance based on the ego-centered consciousness. Summing up the above, this is a mode of consciousness that posits a false image of self, an imagined and idealized "I" that we identify with, and through which we view the world of nature as well as our fellow human beings as Other. As we live life based on our ego-centered consciousness, we become Other to our own selves.

Overcoming the Ego-Centered Consciousness

This way of seeing the root cause of our woundedness in the ego-centered consciousness complements various ways of analyzing the human predicament in some currents of contemporary thought.

Martin Heidegger, for example, pinpointed the basic malaise of Western society in the forgetfulness of Being.[8] By this we can understand the degeneration of human consciousness to a mode that only relates to beings (*Seiendes*), that is, as objects confronting the ego-as-subject, a mode that has thereby lost its connectedness with Being (*Sein*) itself. What is called for is a reconnection with Being itself, the living Ground of our very being, by arriving at a mode of awareness that cuts through the subject-object dichotomy.

In Martin Buber's terms, the distorted condition of our being in the world is the result of the predominance of the I-it mode of awareness over the I-Thou. In rough sketch, I-it refers to that mode of regarding everything in the world as object, out there, confronting the "I" as subject. In contrast to this, I-Thou points to a mode of awareness and way of being wherein I address the universe, in all the particular elements it includes, whether human beings or trees or rocks, as Thou. As I address a Thou from the depths of my being, in an event of encounter that is also a moment of revelation, the "I" is no longer the same as that in the I-it mode of awareness, but is now a transformed self that stands in relation, in the lived awareness of connectedness with the universe at its ground.[9]

These two ways of expressing the human predicament and the way to its resolution are in resonance with the understanding of the roots of our woundedness in our entrapment in the ego-consciousness.

Thus, the key to healing our woundedness on the manifold levels of our existence, including the ecological, social, and personal, lies in overcoming this ego-centered consciousness that controls our attitudes and actions in our everyday life. As we begin to see through this idealized and falsely conceived self with which we identify in opposition to the Other, we hear an invitation from within, to launch into a search for our true self that underlies this delusive ego.

What is this true self? If my true self is not this "I" imagined as in here, in opposition to the world out there, what or who am I?

Answering this question is an issue, or better, *the* issue of paramount importance in our lives. This is also the fundamental question to which the Zen tradition offers us an approach, as it has done over the past millennium and a half of its history.

But before proceeding to our detailed treatment of what Zen has to offer, let us consider two sets of prescriptions for our healing based on different, complementary ways of viewing our situation of woundedness. The first comes from the Buddhist tradition, out of which Zen springs, and the second is the Christian message, which we are engaging in conversation with Zen throughout this book.

FOUR NOBLE TRUTHS: A BUDDHIST DIAGNOSIS

There is a medicinal tradition that derives from ancient India which works on a fourfold set of steps in the healing of a sick person.

The first step involves a detailed diagnosis of the patient, examining the symptoms, the manifestations of sickness, and its extent. If a patient comes with a skin irruption, for example, one does not just apply some balm to it and stop at that, but continues to inquire whether there are other accompanying symptoms, such as other parts which may be hurting, other bodily functions that are not in order.

A good physician does not jump immediately to a treatment that would merely alleviate the symptoms, but rather goes on to the second step, which is the investigation into the causes behind those symptoms. Is the irruption caused by an externally inflicted wound, or is it coming from something else? The patient's diet, sleeping habits, exercise habits, and other elements are looked into as possible factors.

As the causes of the symptoms are pinpointed, the physician goes to the third step, which is the envisioning of a healthy state of being. This is a state wherein this particular skin irruption has subsided and ceased to bring pain, but also wherein the patient is able to go on living in a way that will not lead to further irruptions or other complications, and is able to function normally in daily life.

The fourth step would then call for practical measures to be taken toward such a healthy state of being, to include not only the external treatment of the irruption to prevent its further infection and to assuage its pain, but also the regulation of the patient's diet, sleep, and exercise, and so on. In other words, steps are taken not only to alleviate the particular symptoms or manifestations of ailment, but to address the causes of those symptoms in a way that will prevent their recurrence and enable the patient to go on living a normal and healthy life.

These four steps in healing from the ancient Indian medicinal tradition served as the background framework in the formulation of the key Buddhist doctrine of the Four Noble Truths. This is said to have been expounded by the Buddha immediately after attaining enlightenment, providing us with a key to understanding the nature of that enlightenment, not in terms of thought content, but as a framework for praxis leading to a state of well-being.

The first Noble Truth is usually translated as "life is suffering." This is the Buddha's diagnosis of the ailing situation of human existence. The key word here, *duhkha* (Sanskrit) is much more nuanced than the English word *suffering*. Etymologically, the word *kha* means the hub of a wheel, and the prefix *duh* is something like the English "mis," as when we say something is "mis-placed" or "mis-taken." The word thus points to a situation wherein the hub of a wheel is not properly centered, or is dislocated, and therefore the wheel is not functioning the way it is meant to. In other words, the first Noble Truth is a basic recognition that all is not well with the way we are living our human existence. Along these lines, another ingenious translation that has been offered for duhkha is *dis-ease*, with the hyphen emphasized.

The second Noble Truth is summed up in the proposition that there is a cause for *duhkha*. This proposition leads to an inquiry into the root cause of the ailing human condition, which the Buddha identifies as craving. This craving is in turn pointed out as rooted in ignorance, that is, the state of being in delusion about one's own existence. This delusion is based on the (false) assumption of the existence of an ego, that which is referred to as *I, me, mine,* which is inside myself, which stands vis-à-vis the world out there.

The third Noble Truth affirms that "there is a way to the extinction of *duhkha*." This is understood as the affirmation of the healthy state of being. The Sanskrit word *nirvana*, which is now used in English, literally means the extinction of the flame, and is the key word expressing this third Noble Truth. It is helpful to avoid the stereotyped images associated with this word in popularized treatments, and simply note that it refers to a situation where the basic ailment characterizing our human condition has been extinguished.

The fourth Noble Truth spells out the particulars of the way toward that state of well-being envisioned in the third Truth. It is presented as an eightfold Path consisting of Right Seeing, Right Thought, Right Speech, Right Action, Right Livelihood, Right Effort, Right Mindfulness, and Right Concentration. In following this eightfold Path, an individual Buddhist follower is opened to a life where one is freed from craving, with the dispelling of the fundamental ignorance about the nature of one's existence that is at its root.

This eightfold Path can be understood as the Buddhist prescription for the healing of the ailing human condition. It presupposes the recognition of the basic dis-ease of human existence as expressed in the first Noble Truth, and is geared toward the recovery of a state of well-being, with eight practical steps that serve as a systematic and concerted attack on the root cause of our ailment.

The basic components in the Zen way of life are also contained in the last three Paths, namely Right Effort, Right Mindfulness, and Right Concentration. The first five steps can be seen as preparatory stages to the cultivation of the last three. Coming from the Buddhist tradition, Zen also derives its basic inspiration from this framework of praxis.

SALVATION AS HEALING: THE CHRISTIAN MESSAGE

Where the Buddhist tradition expresses the human problematic in terms of duhkha, the Christian view presents the human condition as one of being in a state of sin, understood as a state of separation or alienation from God.

In the Creation story in the Book of Genesis, man and woman, originally created in God's image, choose a course separating themselves from God's plans and thereby place themselves in a state of opposition to God, as well as to the rest of creation. It is this separation from God and the rest of creation that alienates man and woman from their true selves which are created in the image of God.

An important point must be noted here, in that the starting presupposition of the Christian message is not that man and woman have sinned, but that they were *originally created in God's image*, that is, originally created in a state of grace, enjoying the divine presence in their lives. Following the Genesis story, in whatever way one theologically interprets it, the Fall came, as man and woman ate of the "fruit of the tree of knowledge of good and evil" against divine will, losing their graced status through their own choice. The term widely used to express

Christian understanding of the human situation — original sin — is a gross misnomer that has caused a great deal of misunderstanding and distorted attitudes outside and within the Christian tradition itself. There is need to reclaim this vision from the Genesis story itself, that our original condition is one of being in the state of grace, and not one of sin. In other words, what is "original" in our created being is grace, rather than sin.[10]

But the fact is that, historically and existentially, we now find ourselves in a state of sin, a state of separation and alienation from God, the very source of our life and the source of that original blessing. Such a situation of alienation from God can also be referred to as our cosmic woundedness.

We can understand this state of separation from God as involving three levels. First, the separation from God finds expression in our alienation from the natural world, the world of God's creation. We have come to separate ourselves from the rest of creation, from nature, and we have regarded it as something out there to be controlled, conquered, subdued. This alienation is the basis of the ongoing global ecological crisis we are all facing. The second level is alienation from our fellow human beings, also created in the image of God, an image we are not able to give due regard to as we find ourselves separated from God. In such a state, we regard others as in opposition to ourselves, as competitors, objects, means to our own ends. This kind of alienation from one another is at the root of the violence human beings perpetrate against each other. Third, there is alienation from our very own selves, made in the image of God but unable to reflect that image in our awareness and in our mode of life, preoccupied as we are with our idealized and false images of ourselves.

The various facets of our existential woundedness that we described earlier can also be seen to correspond with our state of alienation, and seen as rooted in the same cosmic woundedness. This is what we have in mind when we say that the human condition is in a state of sin and in need of salvation.

The word *salvation*, a key term for understanding the Christian worldview, derives from the Latin word *salus*, which means healthy and sound, in turn deriving from the Greek *holos*, which means whole. The Christian Gospel, as a message of salvation, can also be understood as a message of healing, one that brings wholeness to our lives.

The Gospel, or Good News, is addressed to us in our cosmic woundedness, proclaiming the Way wherein we can be healed and come to wholeness once again. This is by undergoing a total change of heart and mind, a *metanoia* wherein we experience a renovation of our being as we are reconciled with God, with our true selves, with our fellow humans, and with the whole of creation.

Understood this way, we can see how the Buddhist expression of the human predicament in terms of duhkha, that is, as a situation that is dis-located, dis-eased, out of step, or out of touch with itself, is in basic resonance and in agreement with the Christian understanding of cosmic woundedness.[11]

2.

Taste and See

The Zen Way of Life

We begin our description of what Zen is all about with a look at its four characteristic marks and the threefold fruit that comes to bear in the practitioner's life. This will enable us to see how Zen is not an individualistic, navel-gazing kind of spirituality, as it is sometimes stereotyped, but a way of life and practice that opens to a new way of seeing reality. This new way of seeing is the key to healing our woundedness in the personal, social, and ecological dimensions of our being.

FOUR MARKS OF ZEN

The Zen (Ch'an) tradition distinguishes itself by four marks attributed to Bodhidharma (d. 532), the Buddhist monk from South India credited with having introduced this form of practice and way of life into China.[1] The four marks are enshrined in the following verse:

> A special transmission outside Scriptures
> Not relying on words or letters
> Pointing directly to the human mind,

Sees into one's own true nature, becoming an
Enlightened One.

Special Transmission Outside Scriptures

Zen attributes its origins to the enlightenment experience of
Gautama Shakyamuni, the Awakened One (Buddha, from the
Sanskrit verb *budh*, to awaken). Six years of search and arduous
practice, inaugurated by his coming face-to-face and grappling
with basic existential questions, preceded this experience of
awakening or enlightenment.

It was an experience so powerful and transformative that people around him could notice the difference in his very mode of
being. It is said that five wandering ascetics who had met him
at some point of his search and met him again after his enlightenment experience came to be his disciples, seeking his guidance
on how they could become as he was. His words of encouragement and guidance to those who sought the way, remembered
and memorized by those who had heard it, later came to be
written down, and after his passing these written records were
compiled into collections for future generations of followers.

Communities of disciples grew, and several hundred years
after Gautama's death, people were still writing down teachings
said to have been uttered by him and handed down through
generations of followers. We now have a voluminous corpus of
scriptures, called *sutras*, literally, "strands" (that tie together
points of teaching), which preserve these teachings. Each sutra
opens with the phrase "Thus I have heard ... ," indicating that
the anonymous writer is simply transmitting the words of the
Buddha.

Thus, later Buddhist followers could have access to the teachings of the Awakened One through the reading of these scriptures. These sutras were also supplemented by numerous
commentaries on them written by thoughtful disciples through
the ages, as well as compilations of precepts on the regulation
of life that leads to enlightenment.

The Zen tradition, setting itself apart from this publicly accessible written body of teachings, claims an independent and more
direct access to Shakyamuni's enlightenment. This transmission

is said to have been given in a continuous line through chosen disciples, beginning with Mahakashyapa, the designated successor of Shakyamuni, and down to Bodhidharma, who went to China and continued the line of transmission to the Chinese disciples. Through these the line went to Korean and Japanese Zen masters, and so on, to the present time.

The beginning of this direct transmission is described in the following anecdote, included in a famous collection of Zen episodes (koans*) entitled *Wu Men Kuan* (Japanese, *Mumonkan*).[2]

Once in ancient times, when the World-Honored One was at Mt. Grdhakuta to give a sermon, he held up a flower and showed it to the assemblage. At this, they all remained silent. Only the venerable Kashyapa broke into a smile. The World-Honored One said, "I have the eye treasury of the True Dharma, the marvelous mind of nirvana, the true form of no-form, the subtle gate of the Dharma. It does not depend on letters, being specially transmitted outside all teachings. Now I entrust Mahakashyapa with this.[3]

This anecdote indicates the way the Awakened (World-Honored) One chose his successor, in a direct transmission of his enlightenment, without so many words—in fact, without any words at all.

In the Zen program of training involving years of practice in meditation and koan study, the practitioner, in one-to-one encounters with the master, goes through a series of episodes that depict the concrete circumstances in which the various ancestors of Zen attained enlightenment.[4] In these sessions with the Zen master, the practitioner cuts through boundaries of time and space and places oneself in the very mind of each of the Zen ancestors one after another, so as to appropriate their enlightenment experience as one's very own.

This process is described with the image of the handing down of a precious elixir cupped in one's hands, from master to disciple, down through the ages, in a way that does not diminish the content from its very source, that is, the enlightenment of Shakyamuni himself.

The episodes depicting the transmission through the line of

Zen ancestors are largely based on apocryphal accounts, evidently compositions of later generations aiming to validate their lineages by going back in history. But the significance of this is in the weight given to the assimilation of the mind of each of the successors in the Zen lineage in the one-to-one encounter between master and disciple. Such transmission of the mind is deemed crucial in preserving the purity and assuring the continued purification of the enlightenment experience in those assiduous in their practice. The experience of such encounters with the mind of the Zen successors in these sessions bolsters and grounds what Wu Men wrote in thirteenth century China, in his introduction to the compilation of koans mentioned above. He notes that as one passes the barrier, that is, attains the fruit of enlightenment, one is able to "walk hand in hand with the whole descending line of Zen masters and be eyebrow to eyebrow with them . . . to see with the same eye that they see with, hear with the same ear that they hear with."[5]

In other words, we have here a tradition that places a premium on a firsthand, living transmission that assures the vitality of the tradition itself. Looking at the situation of Zen communities in different parts of the world today, one must of course recognize the human reality of institutionalization that has set in within the various Zen lineages that have survived: in many cases this form of repeated one-to-one encounter has been dropped altogether in favor of more formalized and ritualized ways of expressing succession. It is worth mentioning here that there are some lineages that have found footing in the West that continue to value this tradition of "putting on the mind" of the Zen ancestors.[6]

This emphasis on direct transmission can be likened on a surface level to the notion of apostolic succession in the Christian tradition. The Roman Catholic, Orthodox, and Anglican churches maintain that this is a sign of authenticity of their message, that is, that it goes back directly to the first apostles of Jesus Christ. The comparison stops there, however, as the differences between the two kinds of transmission far outbalance this single similarity. What it does indicate is the importance given in Zen, as well as in the Christian tradition, to a return to the sources, the placement of a criterion for authenticity in the direct connection with one's origins. In the former it is the experience of enlightenment of Shakyamuni, and in the latter it is the original kerygma or proclamation of the Gospel message by the first-generation disciples who walked and shared bread with Jesus the Christ.

Pointing to the Moon

The second cardinal mark of Zen is expressed in the maxim, "not relying on words or letters." This indicates that the fundamental experience at the heart of Zen, an experience which throws light on one's whole being, can never be adequately expressed in discursive or propositional language. Zen understands the role of language to be like a finger pointing to the moon. As the finger catches one's attention, it is easy to be deluded and stop one's gaze at it, or attempt to analyze it from various angles. Yet to do so would miss the whole point that the finger itself is trying to make. It is simply inviting us to look up and behold the moon in its beauty, right before one's very eyes. The finger, in such a case, while intended to help one see that moon, becomes an obstacle to actual seeing. That is why Zen keeps reminding us not to get stuck or hung up on the finger — the words and letters we use — not to rely on them, but at best employ them to help us adjust our gaze onto something they cannot even touch, much less express with any adequacy.

We have anecdotes of Zen monks who burned all their sutras on sudden inspiration, in literal fulfillment of this second cardinal mark. One such example is that of Te-shan (782-865; Japanese, Tokusan), disciple of Lung-t'an (Ryutan), whom we find in the twenty-eighth case of Wu Men's collection of koans, described as holding up a torch and burning all his sutras and commentaries of Buddhist scriptures, with the remark, "even though we have exhausted abstruse doctrine, it is like placing a hair in vast space. Even though we have learned the vital points of all truths in the world, it is like a drop of water thrown into a big ravine."[7]

It is ironical to note that Zen has come out with a considerable volume of literature whose basic message is to tell us not to rely on words and letters. Among these are expressions handed down to us as anecdotes or excerpts of exchanges between Zen masters and practitioners, called koans, meant to boggle the discursive and rational mind and evoke a direct experience.

We also have handed down to us volumes of poetry composed by monks and lay practitioners attempting to give expression to an experience or insight coming out of their practices. In fact, such expression has been encouraged in some lineages, with the practitioner being enjoined to submit a poem or a calligraphic piece in celebration of one's enlightenment experience and each time one successfully passes a koan in the training process. Such expressions, however, are of the kind that reaffirm this second maxim, in that they are hardly discursive or rational, using propositional statements. They are expressions teeming with allusions to the natural world, such as birds, flowers, mountains, and rivers, or even ordinary things like bowls and chopsticks. These are not propositional statements about the nature of truth that can be verified or falsified, but expressions of an invitatory nature. Their purpose is to enjoin readers or listeners to *taste* and *see* or *hear* for themselves and let that world of enlightenment be fully manifest to them in a very direct way.

In the Sanbo Kyodan lineage, where I was privileged to receive my Zen training, those who are graced with an experience affirmed as *kensho** or Zen enlightenment are asked to write a short account of their experience and submit it to the Zen master. The common factor one notices as one reads the accounts that have been made public is that they are irreducible to any uniform kind of expression.

Taking some examples from those included in Philip Kapleau's *The Three Pillars of Zen*, which is based on the practice and teaching of the Sanbo Kyodan in Kamakura, a Mr. K. Y., a Japanese executive, describes a profound experience triggered by the words of Dogen, a thirteenth-century Japanese Zen master, to this effect: "I came to realize clearly that Mind is no other than mountains and rivers and the great wide earth, the sun and the moon and the stars."[8]

Mr. C. S., a retired Japanese government worker, comes to his experience and exclaims, "Oh, it is *this*!"[9]

Mrs. A. M., an American schoolteacher, awakes one night

with a bright "Ha!" and "realized I was enlightened."[10]

Mr. A. K., a Japanese insurance adjuster, writes how it dawned on him, *there is Nothing to realize!*"[11]

A Canadian Catholic sister who practiced with Yamada Roshi for many years and went on to found Zen centers in the Philippines writes that her experience was triggered by words of Scripture, specifically those of John the Baptist referring to his encounter with the Christ: "therefore this joy of mine is now full" (John 3:29).[12]

These examples are given here merely to show the differences in the verbal expressions of the experiences confirmed as those of genuine Zen enlightenment. These expressions come from a direct experience of something that can never be fully captured by the referential meanings of the words used to express them — they are the proverbial finger pointing beyond itself, to the moon shining in full glory, available for all of us to behold, if we only bothered to look or take away the cover from our eyes.

There are certain notions referring to the content of the enlightenment experience which have become the subject of much discussion and speculation. One of the prominent terms in this regard is "emptiness," a translation of the Sanskrit term *shunyata*.[13]

This notion of shunyata has been a focal point of discussion in philosophical and religious circles as a key to elucidating the nature of enlightenment. This is not the place to pursue this discussion, and we can note that Te-shan reminds us that "even though we have exhausted abstruse doctrine, it is like placing a hair in vast space ... "[14]

Yamada Roshi himself often repeated a verse from his teacher, Yasutani Hakuun, echoing this notion in a poetic way: "Not a speck of cloud in the sky, to mar the gazing eye."[15]

While being a helpful warning not to place ultimacy in verbal expressions but to go deeper in the search for the truth in Zen, the maxim "not relying on words or letters" can also serve as a convenient excuse for not engaging in this tedious yet necessary endeavor of clarifying our concepts and communicating through language with other human beings on issues of ultimate concern. An anti-intellectual strand has always been present in the Zen tradition, an attitude that disdains the pursuits of the analytic mind. Maintaining such an attitude can only be reproved as intellectual indolence.

We need only to look at the example of Shakyamuni to see this attitude as a pitfall in itself. It is said that after his enlightenment experience, he was overwhelmed by the profundity of what he had come to realize as beyond all words and letters, and remained for a long period in silence, basking in quiet contemplation. Legend says that he was tempted to remain silent all his life, simply relishing the fruits of his enlightenment, but that he was persuaded by the god Brahma to share what he saw with his fellow beings, lest it be lost for the rest of the world. Ultimately it was his compassion for sentient beings that moved him to speak the unspeakable, and from that moment on, he was ready to expound the inexpressible dharma to those who would listen, using words as skillful means in a way that would point beyond themselves.

One realizes that such an endeavor to expound the dharma is fraught with self-contradiction, in that it is an attempt to express what is ultimately inexpressible. Not relying on words or letters, one must nevertheless use them, and use them well, to be able to communicate with other humans doomed to the use of language — or else one will be consigned to perpetual silence.

To put it another way, the maxim of "not relying on words or letters" as ultimate or absolute also applies to its own self, in that one also must not take *this* maxim as ultimate or absolute.

In certain dramatic instances, silence speaks louder than words. There is a famous account of the lay follower Vimalakirti, with whom disciples of the Buddha engage in verbal jousts in the attempt to capture the essence of enlightenment in words. The whole episode comes to its climax with the thunderous silence of the protagonist overcoming all the arguments of the other disciples. Such is a silence that is not just a refusal to use words in a facile or indolent kind of way, but is arrived at after one has exhausted all the possibilities of the use of words, as one crosses the ultimate limits to which words can take us. Using words and letters to their ultimate, one ultimately does not rely on words or letters.

Further, in Zen, as words serve mainly as skillful means to

point beyond themselves, and as there is an express disavowal of the ultimacy of words and letters, orthodoxy or heresy does not become an issue. What is crucial is *orthopraxis*. This means that the important point in Zen is not what one says or even what one believes, but how one lives—whether one's life and action are marked the by the wisdom and compassion of one who has awakened to one's true self.

This centrality of orthopraxis opens the possibility for persons of differing religious beliefs or affiliations to practice genuine Zen. This is the basic stance taken by Yamada Koun Roshi, who welcomed as Zen disciples not only Buddhists, but also Christians, Jews, and others who professed no particular religious affiliation. He did not require them to renounce their religious faith or affiliation, insofar as it did not present anything incompatible or obstructive of their Zen practice.

Yamada's repeated remark in response to questions on this issue was that in the practice of Zen, the Christian's faith could be purified and enable the practitioner to become a much better Christian, the Jew a much better Jew, the Buddhist a much better Buddhist. He especially invited his Zen disciples who were also practicing Christians, who kept growing in numbers through the years, to express their Christian faith from the perspective of Zen experience, and vice versa, to express their Zen experience from the perspective of Christian faith. This book is a continuing attempt to respond to this invitation.

Touching the Core of Our Being

The third maxim is this: Zen points directly to the human mind or heart. Here the translation "mind" or "heart" derives from the Chinese word *hsin* (Japanese, *kokoro*), a term which refers to the very core of our being.

Zen is not a set of teachings about certain things or certain truths, but an invitation to a direct experience right at the core of our very being, an experience that sheds light on every aspect of our lives. Its very starting point is the fundamental question of life and death that we inevitably ask ourselves, expressed perhaps in different forms, but all coming down to the same question from the core of our being: who am I? What is my true self? How am I to understand myself in relation to the entire universe? What is the meaning of all this? How am I to live my life fully in a way that I can be at peace in the face of death? What is the one thing necessary in this life?

Such also is the questioning that the rich young man presented to Jesus: "what must I do to attain eternal life?" Such is the earnest request of Hui-k'o (487-593) to Bodhidharma when he was finally granted an audience by this bearded monk from the Western regions: "Your disciple's mind is not yet at peace. I beg you, Master, give it rest."[16] These are questions that come from the core of the human being.

The core of our being is what we also refer to in our use of the term "spiritual." In a multivolume series covering different spiritual traditions throughout the world, the common preface to all the volumes offers us a helpful description of the term that serves as a working definition—"the spiritual core is the deepest center of the person. It is here that the person is open to the transcendent dimension. It is here that the person experiences ultimate reality."[17]

Our use of the term *spirituality* takes a cue from this. This word cuts across religious traditions, and different religious traditions can engage one another in conversation as they refer to this dimension of our existence. The spirituality of a given religious tradition is the mode of life issuing from the core of our being, as understood and lived in that tradition. Spiritual life is *life at the center*, given concrete expression in various religious traditions, or even outside any tradition. Zen spirituality is a synonym for the Zen way of life itself, as this way of life issues forth from the center of our being.

In the Christian context, the term spirituality comes from the Latin *spirare*—to breathe. Spiritual life, life at the core of our being, has something to do with the breath—the *ruah* in Hebrew scriptures, coming from a divine Source. This is a significant point on which the Christian tradition can engage in conversation with Zen.

The fundamental question coming from the core of our being is what Zen directly addresses. What is my true self? How can I find true peace? What is the meaning of life? Zen responds not by verbal answers or doctrinal explanations, but by way of an invitation: Look and see! Or, seek, and you shall find! Take up the practice, and your eyes will be opened!

What is there to see? The fourth maxim continues: what one sees is one's own true nature. And in seeing this, one becomes an Awakened One (Buddha).

Seeing One's Nature, Being Awakened

The fourth mark of Zen is seeing into one's very own nature (the way one really is), to become an Awakened One. Seeing the way one really is also means seeing all things as they really are, without distortion or delusion; this is why the Awakened One is characterized as having wisdom in its fullness.

Such a *way of seeing* grounds a *way of being* wherein the joys of all beings become one's very own joy, and their sorrows become one's very own. In other words, the wisdom of an Awakened One is inseparable from compassion, because seeing things as they really are is seeing oneself as vitally interconnected with everything else. The term *com-passion*, to suffer with (as opposed to mere sympathy or pity), refers to a way of being that sees oneself as vitally interconnected with every being in this universe. Suffering with and being joyful with flow naturally out of being awakened, that is, being a Buddha.

Thus the healing of our woundedness is the unleashing of this compassion flowing at the heart of our being. Zen enlightenment is the opening of the eyes of wisdom, which unleashes this compassion and enables it to flow into and become a power in the totality of our lives, informing our way of seeing and transforming our way of being and relating to our fellow beings and to Earth as a whole. Opening the eyes of wisdom in the experience of enlightenment is what leads to the recovery of our wholeness, which is the overcoming of our dysfunctional mode of being, characterized by alienation from the natural world, from fellow human beings, and from our true selves.

These four marks, or cardinal principles, indicate the dynamic and living character of Zen spirituality. Let us now consider its fruits as they come to bear in our life.

THREE FRUITS OF THE ZEN LIFE

The fulcrum of Zen is in the practice of seated meditation (*zazen**). This practice enables three fruits to come to bear in one's life: 1) the increase of one's power of concentration (*joriki*), 2) the awakening to one's true nature (*kensho*), and 3) the actualization of the way of enlightenment in one's daily life (*mujodo no taigen* = literally, embodiment of the supreme way).[18]

Con-centration

With regard to the first fruit, *concentration* here does not mean what we ordinarily associate with the word. For example, we could imagine Rodin's sculpture The Thinker, with his right elbow on his right knee and his clenched hand raised to support his head, as concentrating on some thought or other. This posture shows a person caught up in something, and indicates a state of mind wherein the thinker is distinct from the thought, i.e., the subject from the object. This is exactly the opposite of what Zen is about.

As long as we remain in a state of mind characterized by that subject-object dichotomy, we remain in a state of ordinary consciousness that places the "I" (ego) at the center, and everything else is seen as revolving around it. Other persons, living beings, everything we encounter in our life-world—all these remain objects confronting the subject (myself). With this, even the notion of God becomes relegated to an object out there, with such a state of mind centered on the "I" as opposed to everything else.

Con-centration in the Zen context is a state of mind and a state of being where that separation between subject and object is overcome. It is a state where one comes to be focused at the center of one's being. Another way to describe this state of being would be as one of integration, where all the aspects of my being find their proper place in a unified totality. This state of being brings about a sense of wholeness, as well as a sense of harmony. In other words, the disparate elements of our life are brought together into an integrated whole, as we deepen in con-centration.

The Japanese word joriki literally means the power of single-minded attention. A person in this state of mind is fully present to each living situation in the here and now, able to respond fully with one's whole being to the call of each situation. One is fully present at each moment in whatever one is doing, and not divided or separated from the fullness of the present moment by distracting thoughts or by extrinsic forces, by inordinate attachments that detract from living at the center of one's being. To be in a state of con-centration in the Zen context means that one lives each moment in its fullness, in every thought, word, action, event, or encounter in one's daily life.

The most effective way to come to such a state of being is in the practice of seated meditation, where one makes an intentional stance to put one's whole being in the here and now, in following each breath. As one attains familiarity with this way of being aware of the here and now in seated meditation, this awareness naturally flows over into one's mode of being throughout one's daily life, in the midst of different activities or in quiet relaxation.

Seeing into One's True Nature

As one goes on in one's Zen practice from day to day and deepens in this state of con-centration, there can come a moment, during zazen, or more likely at some unguarded moment in one's daily life, where a sudden flash occurs, and in this flash one is given a glimpse of a dimension that entirely transforms one's whole way of seeing and being. This is called the experience of seeing into one's true nature (kensho), the turning point in the life of Zen.

For now we will simply outline the bare elements of this, as we will address it in greater detail in our fourth chapter.[19] Here I would like to point out that although it is referred to as a fruit of Zen practice, it is more properly a gift, a touch of grace. The effort that we put in, including the practice of seated meditation and the intentionality wherein we place ourselves in full attention at every present moment, is to be seen as the readiness on our part to prepare ourselves for the reception of this gift.

We ourselves place obstacles that block the coming of this event of grace, the gift of kensho. These are our own egocentric attachments, our inordinate desires, or our tendency to be disparate and divided in different directions in our life, and therefore not able to listen with our whole being to that wordless Word, the primal Word from all eternity underlying our existence and that of the whole universe, that is being addressed to us at every moment.

The decisive moment wherein we are able to hear that primal Word may come during meditation, as we make ourselves fully still and attentive. But also, in many known instances, it may come in some idle moment of our daily life when, in a flash, the universe breaks open and we see things as they really are for the first time. This can be an experience triggered by the chirp of a bird, the sound of a bell, the sneeze of someone nearby, the tap of someone on our shoulder, or even a mental image or thought, a memory of a past event or encounter. Whatever it is that triggers the experience, it happens in a definitive moment that is clear and unmistakable, and from that moment on, we are ushered into a whole new dimension.

We enter an entirely new world, but yet we also see that it is the same old world we had been in all along, now seen in an entirely different light. That is, we no longer see from the perspective of a delusive ego looking at everything else as an object out there. In the kensho experience, we see from the perspective of things as they really are. It is like seeing things on a clear day in the noonday sun, where everything stands out in full splendor and glory.

Zen master Dogen, in thirteenth-century Japan, had a phrase to describe these two ways of seeing, one based on delusion, the other on an awakened perspective. "Putting oneself forth seeing myriad things is delusion. Myriad things coming forth seeing the self is enlightenment."[20]

The initial experience of awakening, wherein we are able to get a glimpse of everything as it is without any delusions on our part, brings with it a powerful and stunning emotional impact, characterized by great joy, a sense of exhilaration and liberation, often accompanied by laughter, and even tears. This emotional impact can remain for hours, or even days, and will sometimes make people undergoing the experience seem as though they have gone off the deep end. This is because one sees something so new and exciting, and yet so familiar ("Why didn't I realize this before?") that one is just caught by surprise, triggering the powerful emotional impact.

As the emotional excitement and the spectacular effects associated with the initial experience subside, one is able to reach a plateau and come back to the ordinariness of one's daily life, but now with a crucial difference: one is now able to see through the delusions of the false ego that prevent one from seeing things as they are.

The third fruit of Zen practice is the actualization of that enlightenment experience, the gradual realization of its full implications in one's daily life.

Embodying the Peerless Way

After the experience of seeing into one's true nature, the continuation of Zen practice becomes all the more crucial, to enable the experience to come to fruition in one's daily life and not be simply relegated into a wonderful but past event.

Given the powerful impact of the experience itself, one can also remain in a state of mind called Zen sickness, where one becomes fixated on the startling visions one has had access to. Further, attachment to the emotional effects of the experience, bringing about a longing for their return, can consume a person and make one lose balance and perspective. This is because what one has seen in that one glimpse has been so enthralling and fascinating that it draws one's whole being unto itself.

For persons who have been graced with such an experience, continued practice enables the overcoming of such tendencies and enables that world of the true self that one has caught a glimpse of to come down to the level of one's ordinary daily life and bear fruit in it.

One's Zen practice then becomes simply living in a way that lets things be as they really are, letting every facet of one's life find its concrete place in its light. Zen masters characterize this level of practice, which we can also describe as basking in the miracle of ordinariness, with the wonderful phrase: "when hungry, eat; when thirsty, take a drink; when sleepy, go to sleep." This points to a life of total harmony with one's essential nature, an authentic life wherein one is fully oneself in all things.

What is the difference between such a life and anybody's life, if Zen is just a matter of eating when hungry, drinking when thirsty, sleeping when sleepy? The answer is, indeed, there is no difference; yet there is all the difference in the world.

There is no difference, because the person ripe in Zen practice, just like anybody else, eats when hungry, drinks when thirsty, goes to sleep when sleepy. But there *is* a world of difference, in that the awakened person does all this no longer deluded by a false ego that says "I" eat, "I" drink, "I" go to sleep, and so on. One is able to see through things no longer from the perspective of the delusive "I," nor is one swayed by its inordinate desires or divisive designs. Such a person has seen through that "I" and realizes its nothingness, its emptiness.

In Christian terms, one would be able to say that the pure grace of God is fully manifest as we partake in the ordinary human activities of eating, drinking, sleeping, laughing, crying. With awakened eyes we are able to see the miracle in the ordinariness of our daily lives, replete with a sense of mystery and a deep-felt gratitude for everything, experienced as *nothing but* the pure grace of God.

Having seen through the delusive ego, the person who has awakened to the true nature of things—that each and every thing in this universe is *nothing but* the pure grace of God, given from moment to moment—is also able to see through the false separation of subject and object, wherein the "I" is opposed to the Other. An awakened person is able to see all things as they truly are, in their interconnectedness with one another and with everything else. In other words, I am what I am only *because* everything in the universe is what it is, and each element in this universe is only itself as interconnected with everything else.

Such a direct perception of interconnectedness is what grounds the natural outflow of com-passion: every being in this entire universe is not separate from my very own self. In realizing this, the joy of my neighbor is my joy, my neighbor's sorrow is my own sorrow. Being-with, and suffering-with—another way

of characterizing a life of com-passion—becomes one's fundamental mode of being as one goes on from day to day, doing
the ordinary human activities of eating, drinking, going to sleep,
and so on.

From here on it becomes a matter of steeping oneself more
and more deeply into this awareness of interconnectedness, enabling every facet of one's whole life to be penetrated and transformed by it. This is basically what is involved in the third fruit,
the embodying of the peerless way in one's ordinary life.

With the description of the four cardinal marks and the three
fruits that characterize the Zen way of life, we have presented
a general picture in response to the question, "What is Zen?"

We are now ready to consider step-by-step how such a way
of life opens to a new way of living and of be-ing that can lead
to the healing of our broken humanity and our wounded Earth,
by examining more closely what is involved in the threefold fruit
of the Zen life.

In the third chapter we will focus our treatment on the implications of the first fruit, *deepening con-centration*, as we consider
the art of attuning to the Breath. In the fourth chapter, we will
take a closer look at the second fruit of Zen practice, *the experience of awakening* to our true selfhood, and its implications for
healing our cosmic woundedness. And in the fifth and sixth
chapters, dealing with the unfolding of the third fruit, *embodying
the peerless way* in our daily lives, we will look at how healing is
effected in our personal lives and in our life as a member of this
Earth community.

3.

In Attunement with the Breath

Zen spirituality can be characterized as the art of living in attunement with the Breath. In this chapter we will consider the concrete elements involved in Zen practice, highlighting the first of the threefold fruits of the Zen life outlined in the previous chapter. What is offered here is something in the mode of a recipe, with some added explanations of the different ingredients involved.

One cannot emphasize enough that the actual cooking and, of course, eating, has to be left to the reader putting down the book and buckling down to the practice itself, letting the living Breath lead the way.

This point is important because some readers may have gotten used to reading different kinds of books on spirituality, or on religious themes in general, and getting a nice feeling of being somehow uplifted or even inspired, and yet letting it stop at that—a nice but fuzzy feeling that can last for a short time, but will need another booster from the next book. A recipe has inherent limitations as reading material. It can at most whet the appetite, but it will of itself not be able to provide the nourishment sought for. The proof of the recipe, no less than the proverbial pudding, is in the eating.

ELEMENTS OF ZEN PRACTICE

There are three elements that one is called to set in place as one begins the practice of Zen. First is taking a posture conducive to the practice; the second is becoming aware of one's breathing; and the third is the quieting of one's mind to a point of stillness.

A Conducive Posture

In seated meditation or zazen, one is directed to sit in a way that keeps the back straight, and there are six possible seated positions recommended for this.

1. The full lotus involves folding one's legs and placing the right foot on the left thigh and the left foot on the right thigh, as one sits on a pillow or round cushion. This is the most desirable leg position for seated meditation, as it enables one to sit completely balanced, with one's back kept straight.

2. For those who cannot manage the full lotus, the half-lotus is next best, with either the left foot on the right thigh and the right foot under the left thigh, or vice versa, i.e., the right foot on the left thigh and the left foot under the right thigh. As in the full lotus, one sits on an uplifted cushion to enable the knees to touch and be firmly based on the mat or floor.

3. For those whose bone structure does not allow the legs to be bent in full or half-lotus position, the so-called Burmese position is recommended. One sits on an uplifted cushion, but the left foot is kept under the right thigh and the right foot under the left thigh. It does not matter which is above the other.

4. For those who for some reason cannot sit in any of the three above-mentioned ways, the use of a prayer stool, where one can sit and put one's legs under the stool, enables one to keep a straight back while sitting.

5. A fifth way involves sitting with one's buttocks placed over the cupped heels, in the so-called Japanese seiza or formal seated position.

6. The sixth way is the use of a low chair or stool, where one does not lean but sits on the front part of the chair (using from six to ten inches) and keeps one's back straight.

While keeping one's back straight in any of the above six positions, it is helpful to imagine a straight line running from the ceiling, penetrating through one's head and down through one's backbone, where one almost feels riveted to a straight sitting position.

The hands are placed lightly above the thighs, left palm over right palm, with the thumbs touching slightly to make an oval shape with the entire hand position.

There are two schools of Zen that prevailed in Japan, the Rinzai* (Chinese, Lin-chi) and the Soto* (Chinese, Tsung-tao), and they present some differences in sitting style: the practitioners of the former sit together, facing one another, while those of the latter school face the wall as they sit. The San-un Zen Hall in Kamakura follows the latter mode. The advantage I find in this is that facing a wall minimizes distraction.

In either case, it is significant to note that the eyes are not closed, but kept slightly open, with the line of sight about one yard ahead, or at some lower part of the wall that one faces while sitting. One is not to stare, but simply let one's eyes rest on one point.

There are several advantages to having one's eyes slightly open. Closing the eyes would make one more susceptible to drowsiness or to the barrage of images not related to the practice. Open eyes keep one attentive in the here and now, and not in some amorphous or idealized world of one's own imagining. Still another, and more important, point is that slightly open eyes keep the sense of interconnectedness, of nonseparation of the "I" and what surrounds it.

At this point we must note that though seated meditation or zazen is the fundamental posture of Zen practice, it is not all that there is to it: all the possible postures taken by humans in our daily ordinary life are in themselves expressions of, and are meant to be integrated into, the life of Zen.

In the Chinese/Japanese way of describing the human postures, the following four are given: 1) *gyo* (literally, "going"), or human posture in action, which could be walking, running, or engaging in some kind of activity; 2) *ju* (literally, "dwelling" or "remaining"), or some kind of passive stance, like simply standing at attention; 3) *za* (literally, "seated"), which refers to the seated posture described above; and 4) *ga* (literally, "prostrate"), or the posture taken in lying down to rest or sleep. In other words, in these four possible human postures, one is called to be fully aware of the here and now and realize harmony and oneness with all that is.

With the above duly noted, we must nevertheless point out that formal Zen practice takes its primary form in seated meditation or zazen.

In the Western spiritual traditions, posture does not seem to be a major issue of consideration in meditation or contemplative prayer. We are, of course, used to seeing pictures of saints or religious persons kneeling in prayer, and this seems to be the posture assumed in the Western Christian tradition for human beings to take in the presence of the divine. This comes perhaps from a cultural context where bending one's knees before a higher authority is a commonly acknowledged sign of submission and respect. We note, for example, Paul's comment in the letter to the Philippians, that "at the name of Jesus, every knee should bow, in heaven and on earth and under the earth ... " (Phil. 2:10).

We can only speculate as to the actual posture Jesus took in his own prayer, but based on artists' conceptions, we have mental images of him kneeling with hands folded, or almost prostrate, as in the scene of agony in the Garden of Gethsemane. Standing up is the position Christians normally take when saying the Prayer of Jesus (*Our Father*) together. Sitting down in benches or church pews, when not using kneelers, likewise is a common posture in prayer.

In his *Spiritual Exercises*, St. Ignatius of Loyola makes provision for different possibilities of posture in meditation or contemplation, including not only kneeling, but also standing, prostrate, supine, sitting, walking, and so forth. For example, in his Additional Directions for the First Week of the Exercises, he notes:

> I will enter into the meditation, at times kneeling, at times prostrate on the ground, at other times supine, or seated or standing, always intent on seeking what I desire.
>
> After I have finished an Exercise I will examine for the space of a quarter of an hour, either while sitting or walking, how I have suceeded in the meditation or contemplation.[1]

In other words, there is a great amount of flexibility among Christians on the particular postures taken during prayer. In contrast, Zen is somewhat more directive regarding posture.

As one finds a suitable seated posture, one is ready to turn to the second element, which is attention to one's breathing.

Following the Breath

Maintaining a straight back in a seated position enables one to breathe most naturally. The second point to consider in seated meditation is attention to one's breathing. This is a point that remained generally undeveloped in most Western spiritual writings in their accounts and prescriptions of meditational or contemplative practice, with some exceptions.

The *Philokalia*, for example, contains the following passage:

> You know, brother, how we breathe; we breathe the air in and out. On this is based the life of the body and on this depends its warmth. So, sitting down in your cell, collect your mind, lead it to the path of the breath along which the air enters in, constrain it to enter the heart altogether with the inhaled air, and keep it there. Keep it there, but do not leave it silent and idle; instead, give it the following prayer: "Lord, Jesus Christ, Son of God, have mercy upon me." Let this be its constant occupation, never to be abandoned. For this work, by keeping the mind free from dreaming, renders it unassailable to suggestions of the enemy and leads it to Divine desire and love.[2]

St. Ignatius gives a concrete description of one form of prayer through breathing. In his account of the third method of prayer, he recommends that "at each breath or respiration, (the exercitant) is to pray mentally, as s/he says one word of the *Our Father* or any other prayer that is being recited, so that between one breath and another a single word is said."[3]

Such a way of prayer that involves the recitation of a single word of a well-known prayer with every breath can be an effective way of enabling the practitioner to be steeped in the atmosphere (literally, the circle of the breath) of the prayer itself, not just mentally, but with one's whole bodiliness integrated in the prayer.

St. John of the Cross also experienced the significance of breathing in his own contemplative prayer, as he writes in his *Spiritual Canticle*:

> The breathing of the air is properly of the Holy Spirit, for which the soul here prays, so that she may love God perfectly. She calls it the breathing of the air, because it is a most delicate touch and feeling of love which habitually in this state is caused in the soul by the communion of the Holy Spirit. Breathing with His Divine Breath, He raises the soul most sublimely, and informs her that she may breathe in God the same breath of love that the Father breathes in the Son, and the Son in the Father, which is the same Holy Spirit that they breathe into her in the said transformation. And this is for the soul so high a glory, and so profound and sublime a delight, that it cannot be described by mortal tongue, nor can human understanding, as such, attain to any conception of it.[4]

In the practice of seated meditation in Zen, the breath is at the fulcrum of one's entire activity (and passivity), and with this one is brought into touch with the living core of one's very being itself, a mysterious and marvelous source of power and healing. The fact is, most of us have actually forgotten how to breathe and have thus lost touch with the core of our own selves. Zen practice thus enables us to recover the art of breathing naturally, and allows us to be at home and at peace with our own selves.

Incidentally, in Tagalog, my mother tongue, the word *pahinga*, which means "to let breathe," also means "rest" or "repose." Experienced Zen masters point out that the most natural way to breathe is the way a sleeping newborn baby does: its whole being is given over to each breath in the most natural way. It is this way of breathing that we have to relearn as adults.

For those beginning the practice of seated meditation in Zen, it is most helpful to start by counting one's breath, one with the in breath, two with the out breath, and so on, up to ten, and then start again from one. In this way one is able to harness one's mind and enable it to focus on each breath. This is like making use of a cane or stick to help one in walking if one finds one's feet weak and wobbly.

Or, to take an image from the Philippine countryside, it is like carving successive notches on each side of the trunk of a coconut tree for each foot to hold onto as one attempts to climb the coconut tree. Each notch is like the number that guides the climber steadily on the way up or the way down.

As one becomes accustomed to harnessing the mind to the breath in this way, the counting is modified. One can then count only with the out breath up to ten, and back to one, then up to three and back to one, and then just "one," repeatedly.

The counting of the breath is not to be taken as a mere mechanical activity; in each count, the practitioner is invited to experience the fullness of each here and now. A deep experience of stillness and oneness can also be arrived at as one counts one's breath.

For instance, I recall an account by a participant in a weekend Zen retreat I directed for a group of senior high school students. Since practically all were new to this practice, I initiated them in the preliminaries and recommended breath counting to the group for the entire weekend period. Most of them spent the whole time on this exercise of counting their breath, as directed. At the end of the retreat, when the participants were invited to share what they had experienced at the final gathering, which is always held over tea, many recounted, as expected, their initial difficulties with posture, with pains in the back, with adjusting to the rigorous time schedule.

But one particular student, who also had her share of leg pains, shared how, as she remained faithful to her practice and continued counting, in just one breath throughout all this, she lost herself, was absorbed in, and "just became one" with the number three. This one brief moment became for her a land-mark of the arduous three days, giving her a taste of something entirely new. That moment of oneness with the number three (it could have been one, or two, or ten, but it just happened to come with the number three), was for her a veritable moment of grace, which made all the difference in her appreciation of the practice. Since that moment, for her, Zen was no longer just the rigorous exercise of leg folding and breath counting. It was, of course, this also, but her experience of "becoming one with the number three" gave her a glimpse of that world of inner freedom and interconnectedness that Zen practice opens us to.

As one finds facility with this practice of counting the breath, one may forego the numbers altogether and simply follow the breath with one's mind, as it comes in and goes out. Inhale, exhale, inhale, exhale, and so on. This is now like being able to climb up and down a coconut tree without the aid of the notches for each step, as one becomes more agile in the endeavor.

In other types of Oriental meditation, there are detailed instructions concerning one's breathing and different kinds of breathing exercises. For example, in Hatha Yoga, there is a way of breathing where one uses one's finger to block one nostril and breathe in through the other, and then exhale through the opposite nostril by blocking the one through which one inhaled. These exercises may help to heighten the awareness of the breath from different angles. Some who find these helpful may adapt them in their own preparation for practice, but these are not normally employed in Zen practice, except as individual prescriptions for those who may have breathing difficulties and need additional help being able to get more accustomed to the normal and natural way of breathing.

In sum, the prescribed way in Zen is simply to breathe normally and naturally, but deeply and in a way that is centered on the lower diaphragm, an area called *hara* in Japanese. One breathes—placing one's full attention on every breath as it comes in and goes out—literally with one's whole heart and whole mind. Each full breath is received with a new freshness, lived in each here and now. It is this living in the here and now, focused on the breath, guided by the breath, that will open one to a deeper level of awareness.

Silencing the Mind

As one is able to place one's attention on every breath, each with a new freshness, the third point in the practice of seated meditation naturally takes care of itself: the silencing of the mind. But this third point is actually the most difficult to accomplish and the most troublesome to deal with, taking a great deal of struggle.

Anyone who tries to sit still for a few seconds will find that the mind naturally tends to wander or to entertain one thought or another. That is simply the way it works in our ordinary consciousness: the mind is active in pursuing objects of thought or matter for reflection or rumination.

What we are invited to do in Zen practice is to put a stop to this normal activity of the mind and let this discursive and restless mind come to a point of stillness in the here and now.

Breath counting is a very effective way of regulating one's thoughts, of harnessing them to enable the mind to focus on the here and now.

How then does one deal with stray thoughts? This is the most common question asked by those who engage in meditation of any sort. As for seated Zen meditation, the rule of thumb is to neither pursue them nor drive them away by force. To pursue them or to engage oneself in them is to separate oneself from the here and now, and to drive them away by force will only make them come back with a vengeance. The most effective way to deal with stray thoughts is simply to recognize them as such, and upon doing so, to go back to one's breathing each time one notices one has gone astray.

On this point, a very helpful hint was always given by the late Fr. Hugo Enomiya Lassalle, S.J. (1898-1990), one of the first Christians to have gone deeply into the practice of Zen, who in his eighties, after over thirty years of practice, was given permission to teach Zen to others by his master, Yamada Koun.[5] In the Zen retreats he directed both in Europe and in Japan, he would keep repeating that practitioners should deal with stray thoughts "as Mt. Fuji would deal with the clouds that come its way." In other words, the mountain is affected in no way at all by passing clouds, but simply remains there, unmoved and unperturbed.

This practice of seated meditation, where one does nothing but simply sit, focusing on the here and now with every breath, is the very heart of Zen itself, in its marvelous simplicity. This is what is known by the Japanese phrase, *shikan taza*, coming from the thirteenth-century Zen master Dogen, which literally means "just sitting," or "single-minded sitting," which we will consider again in the next chapter.

In the Rinzai school of Zen, a mind-boggling question or conundrum known as a koan* is used to cut through the discursive activity of the mind and force it to a corner, where it cannot find a way out by using one's rational faculties. More about the koan will be explained later, but suffice it to say at this point that it is one of the devices employed to quiet the restless mind or to put a stop to its discursive function.

A koan, however, cannot be worked on by an individual wishing to practice Zen meditation on one's own. It is meant to be taken up under the direction of an authorized Zen master or teacher who has gone through the Zen experience involving koans. Otherwise it is easy to be misled in this regard, to construe all kinds of possible answers suggested by the many readily available published works about Zen, and miss the mark entirely.

In other forms of Eastern meditation, what is called a mantra is sometimes employed to help the practitioner focus the mind on one point. This is a word or short phrase given by the guru or meditation master to the practitioner, which the latter then is invited to repeat with every breath during meditation. The mantra thus becomes a focal point around which the practitioner can rally one's resources and wherein s/he finds one's own center. Devoting one's attention to the mantra in this way mitigates the entry of irrelevant or stray thoughts and keeps the mind on a point of focus.

There are some Christian spiritual directors who have been adapting the use of the mantra for those they direct in meditation or contemplation, making use of a Holy Name or word or phrase from Sacred Scriptures that strikes a resonating chord in the practitioner. In any case, the use of a mantra can be an effective way of quieting the mind to a point of focus, but how the individual practitioner deepens in one's practice will depend in great part on the way one is guided by an experienced director. A particular koan a practitioner may be given by the Zen teacher can often serve as a mantra in this way, such as the famous koan on *mu,* which we will consider in our next chapter.

THE ZEN TEACHER AS MIDWIFE

In Zen practice, one cannot emphasize enough the vital role of the Zen teacher who has charted the paths of this arduous journey to the core of one's being and is familiar with the terrain. There is a proliferation of literature on the matter that may just leave the individual seeking a handle or practical guide as to what Zen is all about all the more confused. The opportunity to receive guidance from an authentic Zen teacher can make all the difference in getting though the maze.

In this connection, it has been a source of greatest blessing in my own life to have been sent to Japan as a Jesuit student in 1970, when I was in my early twenties. The school I was sent to in order to learn the Japanese language was located in Kamakura, about an hour's train ride from Tokyo. This was also where San-un Zendo, or the Zen Hall of the Three Clouds, was located, and it was here that I had the privilege of being initiated into Zen by Yamada Koun Roshi. Guided by his astute hand and compassionate heart, I was led step-by-step into the inner world of Zen, and in 1987 I finished formal koan training under his direction. There is so much I would like to be able to express and write about in this whole journey to the inner world of Zen, but this will have to wait its due time. As of now, I can only express my gratitude for this privilege of having met and of being guided by Yamada Roshi by carrying out the mandate I have received to carry on the tradition, enabling myself to be of assistance to others wishing to undertake the same journey.

One of the great joys I have been privileged to partake in over the years in helping out in Zen retreats is being able to assist in the process whereby participants are enabled to let go of their baggage and come to a fundamental experience of "seeing into one's true nature," a liberating experience that transforms the individual practitioner's whole way of seeing, of relating, of being. In this process the feeling one gets is that of a midwife who has been of assistance in the birthing of a new life. The midwife is by no means the source of that life, but is simply one who sees to it that the way is cleared and the conditions made favorable for the new life to come through and see the light. Each birth is indeed a joyous and exciting event, filled with a fresh sense of wonder and mystery.

The teacher-disciple relationship in Zen involves a covenant whereby the teacher agrees to render to the disciple whatever is called for or necessary in enabling the disciple to live more fully the life of oneness and interconnectedness that Zen practice opens one to. In turn, the disciple takes the teacher as a person to look to for guidance in such a vital matter as one's journey in encountering the mystery of one's very being. In presenting oneself to a particular teacher in Zen, it is understood that the disciple will take this teacher's word to be authoritative in matters relating to Zen practice and will not turn to other teachers to seek help on the same matters while one remains in this covenant.

This is especially important for those who are beginning in this practice and need a decisive guiding hand to lead them in this rigorous practice involving a perilous process. Going from one teacher or director to another may only confuse the practitioner, as different teachers inevitably have different styles in their direction of others, and there may be conflicting points in the details of practice given to the same individual. To avoid such confusion on the part of the beginning practitioner, it is of prime importance that the disciple follow the guidance of *one* teacher that s/he feels confident in being able to show the way, rather looking for a second opinion on spiritual matters.

However, if the practitioner somehow begins to feel that this particular teacher may not be the one best suited for oneself, then the practitioner is always free to express this, bid farewell to the teacher, and go to another with whom the practitioner can resonate better. Such a case then is not a breaking, but a concluding of the covenant, and the practitioner is then free to begin another one. In doing so, s/he is enjoined to set aside and forget everything received from the former teacher, lest anything stand in the way of full acceptance of the guiding hand of the newly chosen teacher, who inevitably would have a different style of direction.

A true teacher does not make an issue of a disciple's departure and, in fact, wishing only the practitioner's greater good, is ready to help the latter in finding another teacher who may be of better help. The guiding principle for the teacher in such cases is to translate a famous Japanese proverb *Kuru mono wo kobamazu, saru mono wo owazu* ("not refusing those who come, not pursuing those who go").

We are describing the fundamental steps involved in the practice of seated Zen meditation, but this written account can in no way take the place of a living teacher who can guide the practitioner by the hand, step-by-step in the process. This chapter only gives an outline and general idea of what is involved in the practice, for those who wish to begin on their own before they are able to meet a suitable teacher who will be able to direct them toward greater depths. Also, this description hopes simply to whet the appetite of the reader, by presenting in a simple manner the way in which one can attune oneself to the breath, deepening and heightening the awareness of the mystery of one's being. One may be able to follow the instructions in a cookbook, but there is no better way to be initiated into the culinary arts than to have at one's side an experienced chef, such as one's mother or grandmother, who knows just how to get the ingredients together and can point out those little things along the way that make a difference in the taste of the whole dish.

Zen spirituality can be described simply as "the art of living in attunement with the Breath," and it is the Breath itself that will be the most reliable guide in the entire journey. Ultimately, the task of the Zen teacher is to help the practitioner be tamed by the Breath, to be fully given over to its healing and transforming power.

In the Christian tradition, the spiritual director continues to play an important role in the spiritual development and deepening of individuals in their practice of authentic Christian living. The priest-confessor has been one traditional role model in this regard, to whom individual faithful could relate as an authorized representative of the Christian community. The confessor could also serve as a confidante to whom one could bare one's soul in matters of conscience, and from whom one could receive guidance for the progress of one's spiritual journey.

Such a role of spiritual director can also be taken by persons who are not necessarily ordained to a clerical or ministerial function in the church. These could be individuals who are graced with the gift of being able to listen and to be for others something like a mirror by which they can see themselves and their own souls more clearly and objectively.

Also, it is a precious gift to be friends with a person who can be one's spiritual confidante. Such a confidante may not be a director in the proper sense, but the very sharing of one's spiritual life with another person enables one to see some things a bit more clearly than when one keeps them to oneself.

The role of a spiritual director can be especially crucial for an individual's progress in meditation and contemplative prayer. In the *Spiritual Exercises* of St. Ignatius, the role of such a director who is well versed in these exercises is indispensable, especially for help in that very delicate endeavor called discernment of spirits. This is the task wherein one is called to look into the movements within oneself to discern if these originate from a divine source and therefore must be ascertained and given heed to, or from another source that must be shunned. Such discernment is especially crucial in making decisions that affect one's way of life or way of dealing with persons.

REDISCOVERING THE BREATH

It seems most of us living in this fast-paced contemporary society have actually forgotten how to breathe. Not that we have ceased to perform the biological function whereby we inhale this invisible mixture of gases, including oxygen, that we need for sustaining life, and exhale what we don't need, including carbon dioxide, which plants in turn need for their biological life. We do this largely unconsciously, and so we maintain ourselves in our physiological existence without having to be aware that it is happening most of the time. What we would like to note here is that breathing, for most of us, has come to be nothing but that—a mere biological function that our lungs take care of for us as we wake and go to sleep, day in and day out. We have come to take breathing for granted.

One of my earliest memories as a child was when my mother took me to a funeral service held at a house a few blocks walking distance from ours, in my hometown in the Philippines. My mother held me by the hand as we lined up in the living room parlor to pay our last respects to the deceased, whom I gathered was a distant uncle that I did not recall too well in life. As we approached the coffin, I recall being lifted up and made to look very closely at the face of the deceased lying in state. That early face-to-face encounter with death left a deep impression upon me. As we were walking home, I remember asking my mother, as I held her by the hand, "Inay (mother in Tagalog, my native tongue), why do people die?"

As always, Mother had a way of dealing with my troublesome questions, and I clearly recall how she answered me then, without batting an eye, "That's because they forget to breathe!" This answer left a mark on me and left me worried, and I took a deep breath or two right then, to make sure I too didn't forget. I remember how I almost couldn't sleep that night, anxious that I might forget to breathe in my sleep.

This early childhood memory serves as a landmark in my journey toward the awareness of the significance of the breath and its transformative and healing power. It was not until years later, as I came to Japan in my early twenties and began Zen practice under an authentic Zen master in Kamakura, that this awareness took on a new level.

With the three-pointed practice of zazen involving posture, breathing, and mind quieting, one is naturally led to a deeper familiarity with the workings of the breath in one's life. One notices, for example, that as one goes about one's normal activities from day to day, one's breathing varies as the pace of these activities heightens or decreases. One tends to breathe in a shallow and hurried way, for example, as one becomes flustered with the way things are going. As one finishes a task or overcomes some difficulty, one heaves a sigh of relief. Different states of mind occasion different kinds of breathing. Also, as one goes through daily life without paying attention to one's breathing, it is easy to get dispersed into many different directions and feel a lack of a sense of unity or cohesion in one's life.

In seated meditation, with one's back straight, one is enjoined to breathe naturally but deeply, intentionally and slowly, so that the breathing is centered on the lower diaphragm. One thus becomes aware that it is the whole body, not just the lungs, that participates, or rather, partakes, in the breathing. And as one becomes more and more familiarized with this way of breathing while doing zazen, this way of real-izing one's connectedness with the breath flows into what one does after zazen. One finds oneself breathing more easily and with a greater sense of relaxation and satisfaction.

This process of familiarization with the breath is what we experience as we go on in our practice: the connection between our zazen and the rest of our daily life, taking the fourfold posture given above, *gyo-zen*, or Zen in action, *ju-zen*, or Zen in passivity or relaxation, and *ga-zen*, or Zen in horizontal position, that is, even while one is asleep, in addition to *zazen*, comes to be realized more and more.

One helpful way of enhancing this awareness of the connection is by taking advantage of those odd or idle moments in our day, such as while waiting for a red light to turn green at an intersection, while waiting for an appointment, or in the interval that naturally takes place as one goes from one task to another, and during those moments, intentionally taking a deep breath or two, placing oneself in the here and now where one is. As one is able to catch those moments and bring them back to the here and now with the help of the breath, one actually notices the qualitative difference in the way one lives one's day. Instead of losing those moments fidgeting or getting impatient or anxious, one finds that those moments become connectors that tie one's life together, back to the living center where it originates — the here and now.

THE BREATH AS CONNECTOR AND HEALER

Individuals are led to Zen practice by many different kinds of motivating factors, and one of them can be the acute sense of needing to put together the disparate or disintegrating elements of one's life. For such a one, the very practice of sitting in stillness, driven by no external force to perform or "do" anything, but invited to simply be, and be fully relaxed in that stillness, can be a refreshing experience of rediscovering that sense of wholeness one is looking for.

Some observers may question whether such a practice of withdrawing from activity for a while and just sitting in stillness is not a simple escape mechanism where one shuts out the rest of the world and finds a temporary haven of tranquility, without really solving or changing anything in one's life. Some have asked whether such a practice is not just an act of self-hypnosis, a temporary cop-out from the real concerns of the world in turning to a self-induced euphoric state.

One can only respond to such questions by pointing out that sitting in stillness in zazen, focusing one's whole being in the here and now with every breath, is not shutting oneself off from the rest of the world but plunging oneself at the heart of the world by attuning oneself to the vital core where things are happening, right here and now, with the breath. As one focuses on the here and now by following the breath, one "tunes in one's receiver," as it were, to realize one's connectedness with everything else in the universe that is vivified by the same breath.

As I focus on my breathing in and breathing out, here and now, I literally put myself in connection with everything else that is connected with this very breath: all the living beings of the human and animal domain with which I share the air I breathe; all the plants who receive what I exhale and give me oxygen in return, and so forth. In other words, I put myself at the heart of this circle of interconnectedness as I entrust my being upon the breath, from moment to moment. As I do so, I see my actual connection not only with the oak tree in the garden[6] but also with the trees in the Amazon forests being depleted at a rapid pace; with all the green plants in the world that provide sustenance in different ways to the whole earth community, etc. Not that I keep the images of these in mind as I breathe, but that these are all already contained in every breath I take.

Attuning to the breath in the here and now reconnects me to the whole Earth community, as it puts me in touch with my deepest self. As I grow deeper in this practice, I become more transparent to myself and also come to realize that I bear so many wounds within myself: the unhealed wounds of my own past, in my unsettled issues, in my broken relationships. I also come to realize that I share the woundedness of others, not only of my fellow human beings, but also that of the whole Earth.

But as I become more transparent and thus sensitive to this woundedness that I am, and the woundedness that I share with my fellow human beings and with Earth, I also discover that in the very same breath that I breathe, here and now, lies the balm that would lead to the healing of my own and Earth's very woundedness.

We can picture how a mother would gently blow her warm breath over a gash or wound on the knee of her child who has stumbled on the ground, and in a most natural way, assuage it and hasten its healing, comforting the child in the process. In the same way, as I entrust my life from moment to moment to the breath, as I do in zazen, I can actually sense that mother breathing over the wounds of my being, and in some mysterious but quite discernible way, assuaging me, comforting me, and healing me, and also leading me to open the eyes of my heart to my connectedness with the wounds of Earth itself. The opening of the eyes of my heart in this way is the unleashing of the powers of compassion working in me and through me toward all sentient beings with whom I share that breath.

THE BREATH IN CHRISTIAN SPIRITUALITY

Continuing on a personal note, as I gradually came to a deeper awareness and appreciation of breathing in my life with the practice of Zen as described above, my reading of the Hebrew Bible and Christian Scriptures took on some fresh perspectives.

For example, the opening lines of the Book of Genesis introduce the divine Breath (*ruah*) that lies at the basis of all being and all life, that power which gives everything its form and shape. "In the beginning God created the heavens and the earth. Earth was without form and void, and darkness was upon the face of the deep, and the Breath of God was moving over the face of the waters" (Gen. 1:1-2).

As one lives and becomes aware of the very concrete centrality of breathing throughout one's life, such a passage ceases to remain on an abstract level, or as a subject of theological speculation on the level of concepts. Rather, one is able to see in a deeper way and experience, here and now, the cosmic significance of *this* very Breath flowing through me, giving me life, making me what I am, as it also moved in the beginning over the face of the waters and gave everything its form and shape. It is the same Breath that is at work now, in me, and throughout the whole universe.

This same Breath is the power that inspired the prophets to be able to speak the word of God to the community, uniting them under God's covenant, calling them to repentance as they strayed from the path that God intended for them.

As we come to the New Testament, the centrality of this Breath in the whole life of Jesus, beginning with the events that prepared for his birth, until the final moment of his death on the cross, becomes manifest.

For example, John the Baptist, who prepared the way for Jesus' coming and the people's reception of his message, is said to be "filled with the Breath of the Holy One, even from his mother's womb" (Lk. 1:15).

Mary the mother of Jesus is told of the news of her conception with these words: "The Breath of the Holy One will come upon you, and the power of the Most High will cast a shadow over you. Thus the child to be born of you will be Holy and will be called the child of God" (Lk. 1:35).

As Jesus comes to adulthood and prepares for his ministry of the Good News, he is led by the Breath into the desert for forty days (Lk. 4:1) and, purified and confirmed in his mission, comes back to Galilee in the power of the same Breath (Lk. 4:14). Entering a synagogue, he stands before the community and reads a passage from the prophet Isaiah, inaugurating his public ministry with these words:

> "The Breath of the Lord is upon me . . .
> to preach the Good News to the poor,
> . . . to proclaim the release of captives, and sight
>   to those who cannot see.
> To liberate those who are oppressed, and to
>   announce the time of grace of the Lord."
>   (Lk. 4:18)

It is this Breath that empowers Jesus throughout his life and mission of proclaiming the Good News, setting captives free, healing the sick, announcing God's loving grace to all. It is this Breath that is in all that he is and does, up to that final moment on the cross when, having fulfilled his task on earth, he cries out with a loud voice to God, saying "into Thy hands I entrust my Breath"(Lk. 24:46).

It is this same Breath that likewise empowers the disciples, transforming them from cowardly and fearful individuals, ready to retreat back to their fishing nets at the time of Jesus' death, to audacious and confident proclaimers of the same Good News of Jesus the Christ, sending them to the ends of the earth. At Pentecost, this Breath is poured upon the community of followers, the same Breath that empowered Jesus, now empowering that community to be a witness throughout history of all that Jesus stood for, to proclaim to the world the coming of the reign of God in Jesus' name.

To be a Christian, to be a member of that community of followers of Jesus Christ that is the church, is to open one's whole life to that very same Breath, and being transformed and empowered by it, to accept as one's own that mission of Jesus himself of witnessing to the Good News to all throughout one's whole life.

In this sense, Christian spirituality means, literally, life led in the Spirit (Breath) of Jesus Christ. It is a mode of life that "puts on the very mind of Christ" in all that one is and does, as one lets this Breath assume centrality in one's being.

Zen practice brings all this from an abstract and conceptual theological plane down to a very concrete and experiential level in one's awareness, as one deepens in familiarity and intimacy with the Breath in day-to-day life. As I live my life in full attunement with the Breath and let it become the guiding power in my life, I experience the gift of being healed of my own woundedness and am empowered in my own little way to become an instrument of this Breath in its work of healing a wounded Earth.

4.

Awakening to True Selfhood

Those of us who are committed to tasks of social and ecological transformation in our contemporary world find that as we face the multitude of demands brought upon us by such a commitment, we do need to step back from our activities now and then and give ourselves some time for silence and reflection. This is not only to give ourselves respite and take stock of what we are doing and the directions we are taking, but also to touch base with the spiritual resources that can continue to nourish us as we engage in these manifold tasks. For the socially and ecologically engaged, Zen practice can provide such "breathing space" and inner nourishment for continuing in these engagements.

Different persons may be led by different kinds of reasons to begin Zen practice. There are those who are led to it out of some external motivating factor, such as curiosity, through the invitation of a friend that one could not readily refuse, or through some other reason extrinsic to Zen itself.

Then there are those who practice Zen with a view to the physical benefits it can bring about, such as a healthier life, better posture, better circulation, reduction of cholesterol, and so on. And indeed, it has been medically shown that meditation in general does lead to such benefits, so people can come to Zen with this in mind.

There are those who practice Zen as a method of stress reduction, as a way to bring about a sense of inner peace and harmony in one's life troubled by many tensions.[1] Needless to say, such a result does come about from simply breathing deeply and naturally and quieting the troubled mind.

All of these are valid starting points for beginning Zen practice. But whatever initial motivation may have led us to begin, the distinctive thrust of Zen is brought out as a certain kind of question comes to bear in our practice.

THE FUNDAMENTAL QUESTION

At some point in our lives, we come face-to-face with a certain kind of question that strikes right at the core of our being. It may hit us as we are well along the way in life, as in a mid-life crisis, putting into doubt or even overturning everything we may have built up or established up to that point. Or it may come earlier, in one's teens, as one is faced with a multitude of possibilities ahead of oneself, or in one's early twenties, as one takes stock of one's life while being faced with career decisions. "What is the point of it all?" "What is this life all about?" "Who am I?" Or, in a more pragmatic and down-to-earth way, "What am I living for?" Or, one may ask oneself, faced with multitudes of possibilities, "What is the most important thing in life?" This is the kind of questioning that takes us to the crux of what Zen is all about.

Another way of expressing the question could be, "How can I attain true peace of mind?" Here one is referring not just to some kind of temporary state of feeling calm through shutting oneself off from the rest of the world and its turmoils, but to a genuine peace with oneself and with the world that is based on a realization of the true nature of things, that is, things as they really are.

One who begins from an acute sense of woundedness as an individual, in search of personal healing, may pose the question in this way: "Where can I discover the source of power that can effect my own healing?" One who is led to practice out of a need to take stock of oneself in the context of the multitude of tasks demanded of us in the social and ecological arenas may pose it thus: "How can I get in touch with that same source of power that can heal me as well as nourish me in facing my manifold tasks?"

The question may be phrased in different ways, but the common thrust is there: a question that cuts through the core of our being. As an individual brings this kind of question to one's Zen practice or as this kind of questioning leads the individual to Zen practice, the Zen master discerns that such a person is ready to launch into the deep.

There are two modes of practice offered for dealing with such fundamental concerns. One mode is koan practice, and the other is called *shikan taza* in Japanese, translated as "just sitting" or "single-minded sitting." These are two effective ways of helping an individual come to a veritable and experiential discovery of one's true self.

THE KOAN *MU*

A koan consists of an anecdote or episode, in most cases between a monk and an enlightened Zen master, that is meant to cut at the discursive intellect and invite the Zen practitioner to a direct experience from the core of one's being. The practitioner who is deemed ready by the master is given a koan to work with that suits that person's temperament or state of mind. With each interview, the practitioner gives an account of how he or she has grasped the koan or worked with it in practice.

There are many koans that the Zen master can choose to offer to the individual already grappling with the fundamental question described above. Koan practice is a powerful and direct way of grappling with such fundamental questions and being led to their resolution, not in a theoretical or conceptual answer, but in an experience of awakening that is at the same time as liberating as it is transforming.

A classic one offered to many practitioners is the famous koan *mu*. This koan is known to have served countless individuals as the trigger for the experience of awakening.

Here I will briefly present the framework of this koan and provide some observations concerning its implications. The comments I offer here on the practice of the koan *mu* simply follow the tradition of the Sanbo Kyodan Zen community based in Kamakura, Japan, from which I myself derive nourishment and continue to drink.

I would especially like to keep in mind not only those already familiar with the Buddhist terminology and conceptual background involved in dealing with the koan, but also Christians and others who may not be that familiar with many elements of the Buddhist tradition but who are single-minded in their grappling with the fundamental question and ready to take on the invitation to practice Zen in the way outlined in the previous chapters. In the process I will also try to clarify some issues and answer some possible questions Christians and other non-Buddhists may pose with regard to the elements involved in this practice.

The koan is given to the practitioner who presents a basic frame of mind that is not merely concerned with physical or psychological benefits of Zen, least of all to one looking into Zen merely out of some intellectual curiosity or some external-motive, but to one grappling with the fundamental issues of human existence beginning with or represented by questions such as "Who am I?" or "What is the nature of my true self?"

The text of the koan goes as follows:

A monk asked Chao-chou in all earnestness, "Does a dog have Buddha nature?"
Chao-chou replied, "Mu."[2]

It is to be pointed out that, according to a basic Mahayana Buddhist tenet, all sentient beings possess Buddha nature — that is, the capacity to be enlightened. Following normal rational procedures, one could figure that a dog is a sentient being, and from this, would tend to assume that since all sentient beings have Buddha nature, would suppose that Chao-chou should have said, "Yes, indeed, a dog does have Buddha nature." Chao-chou's answer in the original Chinese context appears to be a negation: "No. Not at all!"

So right there the practitioner's mind is tantalized. Why not? Here the practitioner is told, "We are no longer talking of doctrinal matters here. Your mission, should you decide to accept it, is to answer the question, 'What is *mu*?' And the answer must be something that comes out of your practice, and not a theoretical or conceptual one. The answer to the question will open to you your very mind's eye, showing you your true self, revealing to you who you really are!"

This is quite an intriguing invitation, indeed.

In those intensive Zen retreats or sesshin that would normally be from five to eight days, after the practical preliminaries are given on the opening night, the Zen teacher directing the retreat would normally give the first day's Zen talk (*teisho**) on the koan mu, to help practitioners deal with this koan.[3]

A Zen talk is meant not so much to deal with theoretical or philosophical issues that would only lead the practitioner further away from the immediate task but, especially in the context of a Zen retreat, is given in the spirit of the third mark or cardinal principle of Zen, that is, of pointing directly to the core of human existence, dealing with issues of life and death, in order to awaken the seeker's true self.

Thus, after some preliminary comments on Chao-chou (778-897, in Japanese, Joshu) and his style of teaching in Zen, and perhaps some remarks about the key term *buddha-nature* and the warning not to get involved in philosophical speculation on this term, the Zen master would repeat the advice of Wu Men (1183-1260), the monk who compiled and edited the collection wherein this koan is found, on what to do with this koan:

> So, then, make your whole body a mass of doubt, and with your three hundred and sixty bones and joints and your eighty-four thousand hair follicles, concentrate on this one word *mu*. Day and night, keep digging into it. Don't consider it to be "nothingness." Don't think in terms of "has" and "has not." It is like swallowing a red-hot iron ball. You try to vomit it out, but you can't.[4]

An element indispensable in this practice is the one-to-one guidance given by a Zen teacher who has gone through the painstaking process and has continued in Zen practice for years and years. A person with ten to twenty years of experience would still be a starter by Zen standards. To be able to guide others in the practice, this would be considered at least minimal. Such is a person who can thus point out the highroads and inroads, as well as the pitfalls of this journey into the discovery of one's true self.

In this one-to-one guidance given in formal interview sessions (*dokusan**), the practitioner is enjoined in his or her sitting practice to put one's whole being, indefatigably, with every breath, putting everything into this *mu*, even though one is without the least idea of what in the world it could be. Perhaps it could be said that one is in a better position if one actually did not have an idea of what this could be, since one is assured that the point is not to deal with ideas or thoughts or images, but to dispose oneself for a direct experience that would open one's eyes to the reality of who, or what, one is.

During seated meditation (zazen), one is instructed to inhale deeply but normally, and then exhale slowly while uttering quietly within oneself, "Muuuuuuu." In this way every breath is guided by *mu*, and *mu* serves as the knot that ties one's whole being together, enabling everything to fall into place. The very absence of an image that one can attach to *this mu* (except as a distraction for those who cannot help but connect it with the image of a cow making its natural sound) is its advantage over other short syllables or sounds that have a meaning content attached to them.

What zazen is meant to real-ize is not a thought or idea or image about something, no matter how lofty or profound, but the direct experience of the pure fact of be-ing, right here and now, with every breath: a pure fact of be-ing wherein the opposition between the subject and the object is overcome or dissolved (depending on from what angle one looks at it). To focus on something with meaning content would keep one tied to this subject-object mode of ordinary consciousness, as "I" am still image-ing this or that object or idea, as I breathe in and breathe out.

For one whose practice is the koan *mu*, in the walking meditation (*kinhin**) periods between sitting, one is enjoined to take every step with *mu*, continuing to focus one's whole being on this. Further, especially in the context of the Zen retreat, the practitioner is enjoined not to let go of *mu* even for one moment, putting one's whole being into *mu* in everything that one does, from getting up in the morning, going to the washroom, doing one's chores, taking meals, taking a rest, etc. In other words, one is encouraged to take Wu Men's advice literally: "day and night, keep digging into it."

The intense nature of the Zen retreat, where one is given the privilege and the advantage of practicing with a group of individuals sharing the same motivation and where distracting elements that would tend to take one's attention from a single-minded practice (such as business concerns, family matters, and so on) are set aside entirely or at least kept to a miminum, does provide a very conducive atmosphere for con-centration, and can make the difference for individuals in really being able to gather themselves together and literally melt into their practice, that is, melt into *mu*.

The daily (or even twice or thrice daily, depending on the number of participants) interview with the teacher is also a crucial factor in clearing away those elements that tend to be obstacles to the absorption into *mu*. Such an atmosphere can be the occasion for an experiential breakthrough, opening the practitioner into an entirely new world, to "a new heaven and a new earth" (Rev. 21:1).

Outside of the context of a Zen retreat, the individual practitioner is enjoined to set aside a period in one's daily schedule to sit still in the usual zazen posture, breathe, and put one's mind to stillness in the here and now. Usually twenty-five minutes is a normally prescribed time frame, with a five-minute short walk done in a meditative way around one's room, or in a garden, if one has access to one. In this, the prescription is to continue with the utterance of *mu* with every exhaling breath, in a way that *mu* becomes part and parcel of one's very awareness of this breath, of this step, of this movement, and so on. In this way, the distance between the practitioner and *mu* will gradually close in, until there is no longer any space in between. The ripening of practice is when *mu* no longer sticks out as something extraneous to oneself, but has melted into one's very be-ing as one breathes, as one takes this step, as one makes this move. When that melting is complete, one is then able to discover, or better, uncover the answer to the question posed by the Zen teacher regarding the koan: What is *mu*?

The answer that each practitioner discovers for oneself is unique, and can never be repeated by anybody else, and such a discovery is the discovery of one's very own true self.

THE DYNAMICS OF SELF-DISCOVERY

In the introductory talks given to beginners at San-un Zendo in Kamakura, the parable of Enyadatta is offered to give practitioners an insight into the dynamics of discovery involved in the practice of *mu*.

The parable is about a beautiful young maiden who would spend hours before a mirror admiring her own beauty. Then one day, as she looks into the mirror, she is unable to see her own head reflected there. This leads her into deep anxiety and begins a frantic search for her own head. She turns to friends, asking, "Where is my head? What happened to my head?" They of course reassure her, saying "Why, it is right there, where it should be." This bolsters her self-confidence somewhat, but she is still unable to see it for herself.

Then one day a friend gives her a blow on the head, and in pain and surprise, Enyadatta utters "Ouch!" With this, her friends join in pointing out to her, "That's it! That's your head right there." So Enyadatta finally awakens to the fact that her head was right there, right from the start, and is in great joy and exhilaration.[5]

This parable illustrates what happens to the practitioner in awakening to one's true self guided by the practice of *mu*. It indicates that what one is looking for has been right there from the start, but only that for some reason or another it has been beclouded from one's view.

The friends in the parable are likened to Zen teachers or fellow practitioners, who keep assuring one that it is right there, and this reassurance from others bolsters one's confidence, although one has not yet arrived at the realization for oneself.

The actual discovery, or the rediscovery, that it is right there, or here, liberates one from delusions about oneself, and one is now able to live with one's head held upright. Needless to say, this realization fills one with joy and exhilaration, often accompanied by laughter at oneself for having been so dense and stupid and not seeing it before, when it was right there all along. It can also be accompanied by tears of joy that one has now truly come to one's own.

In one sense, there is nothing new here at all. What one is looking for has been right there all along, from all eternity, one might say. Yet in another sense, everything is new. One is now able to see everything from an entirely different perspective, that is, from a standpoint no longer centered on one's ego as subject in opposition to everything else in the universe regarded as object.

From this new perspective attained in the experience of true self-realization, the subject-object division is overcome, and one is enabled to grasp clearly what the Buddhist Wisdom sutras talk about as they point out that there is "no seer, no seen; no hearer, no sound."[6]

The philosophically inclined reader might at this point look for a further theoretical explanation of this perspective, this domain that has now crossed the subject-object dichotomy, which one enters with the experience of Zen awakening. This is what numerous works in Buddhist philosophy attempt to do.

Many of these are especially centered on the inquiry into a key term employed to describe this realm, that is, *shunyata*, usually translated as "emptiness."

There are many written works that treat this notion and its experientially suggestive implications.[7] Rather than engaging in this kind of inquiry in a speculative manner, we will simply point out that the structure of the enlightenment experience in Zen presents itself not as the arrival at something new or the attainment of a state that was not there before, but simply the recovery—or perhaps better—the un-covering, of something that has been there all along.

This is along the same line as what the philosopher Martin Heidegger pointed out regarding the way we humans come to truth or the way truth comes to us, in his analytic interpretation of the term in its Greek form, *aletheia*, which involves an un-covering (German, *Ent-deckung*).[8]

Those familiar with the poetry of T. S. Eliot will also recall the lines from his "Four Quartets":

> We shall not cease from our explorations
> And the end of all our exploring
> Will be to arrive where we started
> And know the place for the first time.[9]

HEARING THE WAY

The experience of awakening that is at the heart of Zen is not an attainment, properly speaking, but can be described as an event that happens, given the ripeness of the conditions that lead to it. It is not the end-product or result of one's effort of seeking or of practicing assiduously. We can say that it is simply a "letting be" of what is, as the obstacles that prevent this are taken away.

This is the way to understand the indefatigable effort that is called for in the practice: not so much as to bring about the enlightenment experience as its result, but as doing one's part in removing those things that block one's seeing things as they really are.

The greatest block to this is our very own ego, the very notion of "self," the "I" imagined as in here, as opposed to objects in the world out there.

Zen practice whittles away this notion of ego little by little and shows it its true place in the universe. That is, ego is totally emptied of any real content. Once this self-emptying is complete, then everything will manifest itself in the way things are.

Here I recall a true story concerning a Japanese lady in her sixties, a story told by Yamada Roshi in one of his Zen talks. This lady had been stricken with a physical ailment which led to her prolonged hospitalization. She had been in her hospital bed for maybe a couple of weeks, and was struggling with the great physical pain that accompanied her ailment. One particular night, she was unable to fall asleep due to the pain and continued to lay in bed with her eyes open. All through the night, there was nothing that she could do but lie there, gazing at the wall, as the sound of the wall clock kept on going, *tick tock, tick tock, tick tock.*

Then all of a sudden, toward the wee hours of morning, without knowing why, simply continuing to hear *tick tock, tick tock* . . . , she was overcome by a deep feeling of peace and exhilaration, accompanied by tears of joy and gratitude, with a sense of acceptance of herself and her pain.

Relatives and friends who visited her the next and following days noticed the great difference in her attitude and bearing, in the way she was at peace with herself and was more open and sensitive toward others. As they pointed this out to her, she related to them this sudden experience triggered by the *tick tock, tick tock*, which somehow was the turning point in this whole change manifested in her mode of being.

Hearing this, one of her friends, who was practicing Zen under a teacher who was a friend of Yamada Roshi's, suggested that she visit this Zen teacher to have her experience checked in the Zen way. Upon leaving the hospital, she did as suggested, although she herself had not been a regular practitioner before. Sure enough, given the usual checking questions concerning Zen experiences, the Zen master confirmed that what occurred in her was a genuine experience of realization.

It may be significant to note here that this lady was not at all predisposed with an intentional attitude of asking the basic question of "Who am I?" or "What is my true self?" and so on, and going into intentional meditative practice with this questioning in mind. One could even say that she was not explicitly seeking answers to these questions, although of course one cannot preclude her concern with basic issues of life and death, with the meaning of her very own life, the question of human suffering, given her particular situation of prolonged suffering.

Having had to live with her physical pain, having had to lie quiet in a hospital bed in patience and long-suffering, was for her a process of inner purification, wherein her ego was mellowed and became more and more transparent, given the circumstances she was placed in. The *tick tock, tick tock* during that crucial night simply served as the trigger that enabled her to discover the realm which undercuts the separation of the hearer and the heard, that realm of interconnectedness that we are, wherein the whole universe is grounded.

The experience of enlightenment in Zen involves the overcoming of this dichotomy created by our ordinary conscious mind between the hearer and the heard, the seer and the seen, between the subject and the object.

A koan offered to help bring about this overcoming of the separation of hearer and heard is the one called *Kikunushi*, or "The One that Hears." With this koan the practitioner is simply invited to find the answer to the question, "Who is the One that hears?" or more succinctly, "Who hears?"

To arrive at the answer, one is enjoined to simply sit in the normal way prescribed in zazen and listen. Not to listen to something that is out there, or in here, in a way as to reinforce the distinction between the listening subject and heard object, but to simply *listen*.

As one is able to place one's whole being in the listening, without any speck of distracting thought or mental image, in a way that one can see the clear blue sky "without a speck of cloud to mar the gazing eye," one is disposed for the momentous event of hearing the timeless word, the word that was there in the beginning, the same word that will be there even beyond the end of all time (see John 1:1-18, Eph. 1:3-10). The hearing of this primal word addressed to one's being from all eternity, a hearing that occurs in this concrete here and now, is the transforming event that bridges one's state of separation of God and thereby heals one's cosmic woundedness.

Such an event—such a gift—of being able to truly hear, even for one instant, makes fully manifest the One that hears, as not separate from the word that is heard.

This reminds me of a famous saying of Chinese origin that Japanese students meet in their junior high school textbooks: "Hearing the Way in the morning, one is ready to die at dusk." This bit of Oriental wisdom points out how the hearing of the way (Tao) is what life is all about, and this event of hearing is the fulfilment of one's whole life. To hear the way even once in one's life enables one to meet death with equanimity, having thus known life in its fullness.

Lest would-be practitioners get sidetracked in mistakenly expecting the hint of an answer in written form here, let me stop at the above description and leave the rest to the actual practice.

To summarize, it is simply bracing oneself, putting one's whole being in the here and now, disposing one's whole self to be able to truly listen, and let the way manifest itself, right there where one is.

SINGLE-MINDED SITTING

The case of the Japanese lady described above serves as a helpful indication that not all arrive at the experience of enlightenment or self-realization with the same conscious frame of mind or intentionality. Guiding many different kinds of persons in Zen practice also makes one fully aware of this fact. Although it can be said that, for a great number, a conscious wrestling with those basic questions of one's identity or questions of life and death is a characteristic note of their practice, for others it is more a matter of putting order in one's life, finding one's bearings, or coming to a centeredness in all that one is or does.

For such persons, zazen is a powerful practice that leads naturally to finding one's ground, coming to a centeredness at the core of one's being, which flows into all that one does.

For such persons, the fundamental question ("Who am I?" "What is this all about?") may not be so much in the foreground of their consciousness as in the background, as an underlying presupposition of their practice. For such a person, rather than offering the koan *mu*, which involves an active pursuit of the question guided by the koan, a most effective way of practice would be what is called *shikan taza*. This is a Japanese compound that means "single-minded sitting," "just sitting," or "simply sitting through and through."

This way of sitting practice may appear to be easy enough, but it is actually the most refined and most difficult. This is incidentally also the kind of sitting normally done and continued by those who have already passed the initial barrier of the experience of awakening, those who have somehow come to a glimpse of that world of enlightenment and are now deepening themselves in its realization in their day-to-day life. For those who may not have necessarily crossed this threshold of the enlightenment experience, this mode of "just sitting" is a powerful form of practice that is goal-less and is an end in itself, embodying and manifesting in its very practice the world of enlightenment.

The Zen master Dogen, who established the Soto* Zen school in Japan after having received its transmission in China, speaks of the oneness of practice and enlightenment, pointing out the inseparability of the two.

Q. Zazen may be an effective way of practice for those who have not yet realized enlightenment. But what about those who are already enlightened?

A. It is said that we should not relate our dreams in front of fools or give oars to woodcutters, but I will try to answer your question. It is the view of the non-believers that practice and enlightenment are not one. But practice is itself enlightenment, and even the initial resolve to seek the Way already contains complete and perfect enlightenment. There is no enlightenment apart from practice. It is very important to realize this. Since practice is enlightenment, enlightenment is without end and practice is without beginning.[10]

In the above, Dogen makes the important point that Zen, which for him finds its quintessence in the practice of shikan taza or "single-minded sitting," is not something done as a means to an end. The practice of zazen or seated meditation in this way is not for the sake of attaining enlightenment, that is, a goal, but is itself the very *manifestation* or *embodiment* of that state of enlightenment as such, the world wherein all things are just as they are.

In philosophical terms, we can also say that this is the world where do-ing and be-ing are no longer distinct, but are in complete and perfect oneness. One sits, and just sits, breathing in and breathing out, and nothing else, with no purposiveness or goal-orientedness. One embodies the simple fact of be-ing, right in one's very sitting. One's very existence right there, in its totality, flows from pure be-ing itself, coming to self-realization.

Right in that very pure fact of "just sitting" is the manifestation
of the true self, just as it is, as flowing from pure be-ing, and
thus as connected with everything else that issues forth from the
same be-ing itself.

But this is not limited to just sitting, either. As one realizes
this full manifestation of the true self in "just sitting," the same
manifestation continues as one stands up and begins walking
meditation. The same thing is true as one proceeds from meditation to the different activities of one's daily life. Each and
every facet of one's twenty-four-hour day can be experienced as
the manifestation of the true self, flowing from pure be-ing—
getting up in the morning, washing one's face, taking breakfast,
driving to work, and so on.

But the difficulty with us human beings is that we tend to get
bifurcated in our ordinary (ego-centered) consciousness—separating our be-ing from our do-ing and also making distinctions
between myself as subject and everything else around me
(including other living beings) as objects—and assume that this
separatedness is the way things are.

What we are awakened to in Zen practice is precisely the
world that overcomes this separatedness, the world of interconnectedness, where everything is realized as such and my self is
realized as not separate from everything that is.

In other words, the practice of "just sitting" in Zen flows into
every facet of our whole life, and we are able to experience
things just as they are, in just walking, just taking breakfast, just
driving to work, just laughing, just crying —"without a trace of
cloud to mar the gazing eye."

This embodiment of the world of enlightenment in Zen, the
world "just as it is," with every breath, with every step, with
every smile and every tear, is replete with wonder and mystery
at every moment.

All this sounds so simple, so hard to believe, and the invitation is to simply come and taste it for ourselves. So Zen practice
is an invitation to a feast, addressed to anyone and everyone.
This is a feast that is a celebration of be-ing, and in it we are
able to join the dance of the universe, every moment of our
lives, in everything we are and everything we do.

It is only our delusive ego, the misleading notion of the "I" thought to be in here, that tends to separate itself from every-thing else, as it were, standing off from everything, as it takes everything else as objects separate from itself, which prevents us from being fully in that celebration. So the invitation is to let go of this ego, unmasking it for what it is, a nonentity. We are invited to empty ourselves of its sway on us.

This letting go, this unmasking of the ego, this total emptying, is what happens in the Zen awakening experience. I am thus liberated from my attachment to that delusive ego, seeing it for what it is—that is, nothing to be attached to at all, something empty. Conversely, in seeing through the ego as empty, I see all things in the universe in full relief without the mediation of this ego, but *just as they are*—that is, in their mutual interconnect-edness and their inseparability from what I myself truly am.

COSMIC AFFIRMATION: GOD IS LOVE

Another account of an experience of coming to this awak-ening may help elucidate a further facet to it. Here I present an extended quote from an account by M. R., a young German woman born and raised in the Catholic tradition who came to Japan for graduate research and practiced Zen at a temple in Kyoto and later under Yamada Roshi in Kamakura.

I had started doing Zen in Germany with Father Lassalle, a Jesuit priest. He gave me this koan *mu*, and hinted to me that the answer to this koan points to oneself, to the answer to the question, "What is your self?"

In Kyoto I went to practice Zen in a temple, and would go to this old master for interviews like three times a week during evenings, and I would bring to him my answer to the koan. At every interview he would simply shake his head, and often he didn't even say a word, and so I would go out and feel very depressed, and sometimes even angry. This went on for about a year.

Then Father Lassalle had a *sesshin** in Tokyo, and I joined that one, in the summer of 1987. During this time, as I was sitting there, practicing with my koan *mu*, some voice told me, *God is Love.*

Somehow for me there was this big question, if God is love, then how come I don't experience this? So I was fighting this voice. It was like fighting the koan *mu*, because I knew, I didn't experience *mu* either. So I was sitting there, fighting *"God is Love, mu," "God is Love, mu,"* and then suddenly I felt a terrible sense of being sorry, a sense of repentance. There I was, the most stupid being that had ever been on earth, for ever doubting that *GOD IS LOVE.*

And then the answer was there completely! I mean, it was not a word or anything like that. Maybe you can describe it like, being touched by God. And it is a really real thing to experience it. So I jumped up and I knew the answer to my koan, and rushed to the interview room and I said, "this is it."

And he (Fr. Lassalle) said to me, "How did you know?" And he confirmed that it was the right answer.

But the interesting thing is that when you find the answer for yourself, you experience it as if everybody else did experience the same thing, because you know it is the same reality for everyone else. And yet everyone else is just as stupid as you in not knowing. From this sense that you feel so stupid yourself, there comes that deep sense of compassion with all the other stupid beings who are so full of grace and full of God's love and yet just like you yourself are fighting against it. This is the way I would describe my experience, confirmed later by Yamada Roshi.

What is noteworthy here is that the experience recounted by M. R. is triggered by a phrase so familiar to Christians, yet for so many it is a phrase that carries a hollow ring. Hearing the words "God is love" evokes many different things in many of us, from a sense of assurance and comfort to a sense of doubt and even positive rejection: "If God is love, how can there be so much suffering and evil and hate in the world? How can God allow such a situation of misery for many, and of continuing destruction of God's own creation?"

It is only when these words cease to be mere words, just as when *mu* ceases to be merely *the meaningless sound mu,* but melts in with our whole being, that it dawns on us: "This is it!"

The Zen awakening experience has to do with the dawning of "This is it!" in our lives. Again, not the words "This is it!" but a true experience that can never be expressed with any words at all (to caution astute practitioners who may read this and simply repeat it in their Zen interview as an attempted answer: no, the mere words will not do), so it might as well be "This is it!" This is an experience that has the power to overturn our whole being, pulling the rug from under our delusive ego that keeps fighting and resisting the reality that we are, the reality that *God is Love.*

In this connection, Paul Tillich has a remarkable essay entitled "You Are Accepted" that resonates with this kind of experience.

Tillich writes of our human situation of sin as the state of separation from the Ground of Being, as well as from one another.[11] In this state of separation, nothing that we can *do* can bridge that chasm that separates us from our very Ground. Any attempt or effort on our part merely widens the gap, as such efforts issue from our egoistic desire to justify ourselves, to "do good" in a way that would make us "feel good" and have a reason for self-complacency. As we are able to admit we are in such a state of separation and realize our very powerlessness in it, we open ourselves to the pure touch of grace in our lives: a voice whispers to us from the depths of our being, "You are accepted."

What we are called to do is nothing but "simply accept the fact that you are accepted!" This opening of ourselves is what enables the reality of the Good News to come home to us and transform our entire lives: "This is it!" And we know, from every pore of our being, the reality that *GOD IS LOVE* is not a hair's breadth apart from the very reality that we are.

"You are accepted." This is a message of cosmic affirmation constantly being addressed to us from all eternity. As we stop resisting with our proud egos and simply accept this fact that we are accepted, just as we are, a new dawn breaks in our lives.

THE TREASURE IN THE FIELD

The dawning of this dimension in our lives, as we cease resisting and simply let go of our whole being, to give in to the reality that we are and that is expressed in the phrase *God is Love*, the reality that I am accepted in the universe by that very love which makes the universe what it is, is our joyous discovery of the treasure in the field described in the Gospel of Matthew. "The reign of heaven is like treasure hidden in a field, which someone found and covered up. Then in one's joy one goes and sells all one has, and buys that field" (Mt. 13:44).

To sell all that we have is to empty ourselves fully of everything that stands in the way, beginning with our ego. It is when we have "sold everything" pertaining to this ego that we are enabled to make that field, and its treasure, our very own.

Having emptied ourselves of our ego that separates us from the rest of the world, we are finally able to come home to our very own. We are at home in the universe, right where we are. This at-home-ness is accompanied by a deep, deep peace, the kind of peace that no one can ever take away.

Zen practice from this point on leads simply to the deepening of the realization in one's day-to-day life, as one gets up in the morning, washes one's face, takes breakfast, goes to work, takes a rest, laughs, cries, yawns, and so on. In all these mundane realities, one's eyes are opened to the unfathomable dimensions of that treasure that is the field itself, re-discovered and now re-cognized as the embodiment of one's true self.

This rediscovery of my true self is the awakening to the fact that I am not separate from the totality encompassing everything that is. This realization is what closes the fissure that divides me from my fellow sentient beings, from the mountains, rivers, the trees, the birds of the air, the fish of the sea, the great wide Earth. The closing of this fissure is no other than the experience of realizing our interconnectedness with everything in this universe, encompassed by the same experienced reality that *God is Love*. In other words, in our awakening to our true selfhood lies the key to the healing of our cosmic woundedness, a healing that will make itself felt in every aspect of our lives from day to day.

5.

Embodying the Way

Zen spirituality culminates in the actualization of the awakening experience in our day-to-day life. This is also called "embodying the peerless way." The following koan captures what is involved in such a way of life.

A monk said to Chao-chou, "I have just entered this monastery. Please instruct mc."
Chao-chou said, "Have you had your breakfast?"
The monk replied, "Yes, I have."
Chao-chou said, "Wash your bowls."
The monk understood.[1]

Let us now examine this koan to elucidate key aspects of the Zen way of life and how it relates to our healing.

ENTERING A MONASTERY

Our starting point is the earnest request of a novice monk who has just entered the monastery: "Please instruct me."

We are invited to put ourselves in the shoes of the novice monk, to be able to see what the koan is about. First of all, we must note that entering a monastery involves a major decision in one's life, whereby one sets aside worldly pursuits of wealth, power, and fame and gives oneself wholeheartedly to the One Thing Necessary.

The subject of the koan is one (you and I) who has taken this step of setting aside all secondary pursuits and has disposed oneself to the realization of what really matters in life. Nothing less than such a great resolve, which includes a readiness to be totally transformed and to live one's whole life in accordance with the demands of one's true self, will be adequate to the issue.

In the original context of the koan as it was formulated in China, entrance into a monastery was the concrete sociological mode available whereby one gave oneself to such a single-minded pursuit. Almost all of the koans offered in the Zen tradition are taken from episodes and anecdotes in the life of monks. Koan study places us within a community of persons who have given themselves wholeheartedly to this pursuit of truth, cutting through time and culture, and we are called to assume a state of mind no less than the single-minded pursuit of truth, or in other words, the realization of true self.

There are, of course, those of us who actually enter a monastery to dedicate ourselves to a religious pursuit, either for a limited period or for an entire life. There are still many Zen monasteries with active communities of practicing monks (male and female) in Japan, Korea, and Taiwan, and Theravada Buddhist monasteries abound in Thailand, Sri Lanka, and Burma.[2]

Also, notwithstanding persecution from Chinese authorities, the Tibetan Buddhist tradition continues to be kept alive in its monasteries peopled by devout and learned monks both in and out of Tibet. China itself had flourishing Buddhist monasteries throughout its long religious history, until the proscription of organized religion, which included destruction or dissolution of both Buddhist and Christian monasteries by the Communist authorities.

A mode of life similar to that found in a monastery could be found in ashrams in India. There one could live a simple life with a supportive community bound together by common spiritual pursuits.

In the Christian tradition, monastic life has always been an esteemed path, and although the numbers of those who enter Christian monasteries and religious orders have been dwindling in the past two or three decades, such a mode of life continues to be a valuable fount of spiritual resources for the worldwide Christian community.

In addition, monks from different religious traditions have begun to invite one another to live for a short period of time in their monasteries, thus engaging in an interreligious monastic dialogue of life. For several years now, Zen monks from Japan have been accepting the invitation to live for short periods in European Christian monasteries, and have invited Christian monks to join them in their Zen temples in Japan. Similar ventures are also being undertaken in the United States, under the auspices of North American Board for East-West Dialogue. These contacts involve monastics of the Benedictine, Trappist, and other orders on the Christian side, and Tibetan and Zen monks on the Buddhist side, as well as those coming from the Hindu tradition, in mutual exchange and dialogue of life.[3]

In different places, experiments in modified forms of monastic living, involving not only male and female celibates but married couples with their families as well, are being undertaken, wherein the members are attempting to forge a way of life in community that would be mutually supportive of their common pursuit of truth, social justice, and a simple and ecologically sound way of life.[4]

In the above koan, we are called to put ourselves in the place of the person who, having just entered a monastery, is now disposed to give oneself wholeheartedly to the pursuit of truth and the fullness of life.

The practitioner (you and I) who takes on the koan need not be one of those privileged ones able to follow the path of monastic life in the literal sense. What the koan does demand, however, is no less an unrelenting dedication to the truth, a single-minded attitude of giving oneself fully in the pursuit of one's true self, as a matter of prime and ultimate concern. We may not all be called to the monastic life, but we are all called to awakening to the truth of ourselves, an awakening to the mystery of our very existence here on Earth, and Zen is concerned with nothing less than this.

In other words, genuine Zen practice is not some kind of hobby or spare-time activity for one's physical or psychological health, in the way that one might take up aerobics or some form of yoga exercise for health and overall well-being. Of course, many individuals can start out in their practice with such an initial motivation. But as one grows in the practice, one finds out that Zen challenges one's entire life, an endeavor that concerns matters as serious as life and death itself. This is the whole presupposition in the monk's earnest request: "Please teach me." That is, "Please teach me not only the rubrics of the monastic way of life, but all about the basic mystery of what life is all about. That is what I am here for."

HAVING BREAKFAST

Chao-chou's response is curt and to the point. "Have you had your breakfast?"

Perhaps I should note that the question, "Have you had your meal?" is also a form of greeting in China. But here Chao-chou is not just making a casual greeting. Recall that Zen koans are always about matters of ultimate concern, the very basic questions of life and death. Someone may ask, "How can such a trivial and ordinary matter as taking one's breakfast be a matter of life and death?" And this is the first checkpoint of the koan, which can be posed in exactly these same skeptical words: "How can such a trivial and ordinary matter as taking one's breakfast be a matter of life and death?" The practitioner's mode of awareness is being challenged here.

Zen Master Chao-chou is not simply giving the novice monk a casual greeting, making small talk, or exchanging pleasantries. He is hitting right at the heart of the matter itself, the basic mystery of what life is all about, in asking the question "Have you had your breakfast?"

This question can be taken as veiled Zen talk, asking, "Have you met your true self?" or, "Have you become awakened?"

The implication, of course, is that if one has not yet "had one's breakfast," then one ought to, without further ado. Zen practice provides a clear and systematic set of guidelines for "having one's fill." In other words, Zen offers a recipe to prepare the meal, and good company to do so. The three main ingredients are: a posture conducive to stillness, awareness of one's breathing, and quieting the mind in focusing on the here and now. Setting one's daily life in order to help make it conducive to one's practice helps in that preparation.

Every person would each have a unique way of engaging themselves in the matter. For some it may be a matter of several weeks or months, for others, years and years, of putting these above ingredients together in one's own way, before one can actually get a real taste of what this breakfast is all about.

In the process, it would make a crucial difference if one had access to the guidance of an experienced cook who has been through it and knows what the taste is like and the different ways of arriving at it, whom one could consult on a regular basis about what is going on as one tries one's hand at cooking. Such a person would be able to point out if the going is right, if there are a few things that need further adjustment, or how one can balance the elements involved, besides showing where one can be sidetracked in the process, and so on. This is what true Zen teachers are for, and meeting such a teacher can make a difference in one's entire life. (I bow again in gratitude repeatedly to my own teacher, the late Yamada Koun Roshi, who in his own lifetime gave himself totally and unreservedly in the guidance of those who sought his help in Zen practice.)

The third chapter of this book, dealing with the essentials of Zen practice, and the fourth, describing the pivotal experience of enlightenment, have tried to present an approach to Chao-chou's question—that is, the way to go about taking one's breakfast Zen style.

One point of interest to note here is that in order to have one's fill in Zen, one needs to *empty oneself*—to empty one's bowl that may have been filled with rubbish accumulated over the years based on a delusive mode of thinking and an inauthentic way of living.[5] This is what the practice of seated meditation or zazen and the intentional way of living daily life in attunement to the present moment as guided by the breath is meant to bring about in us.

"Have you had your breakfast?"

"Yes, I have," was the monk's answer to Chao-chou's question. The monk has been doing his homework. As in other koans, with just one reading, one may get the impression that it is all a piece of cake, or perhaps a bowl of oatmeal. But there is much that goes behind the monk's answer, in terms of the preparation of the ingredients and the actual cooking, then setting the table, and then the actual partaking of the meal itself, before one can say "Yes, I have (had my fill)."

Another koan where an answer given in response to a crucial leading question seems to be all so simple but actually presupposes a tremendous amount of practice is the one entitled "Bodhidharma and Peace of Mind." Here the founder of Zen (Bodhidharma), having come from India into China, is earnestly sought by the man who was destined to become the Second Ancestor of Zen in China (Hui-k'o, 487-593), already approaching middle age at the time of this encounter.

> "Please, sir, your disciple's mind is not yet at peace. I beg you, my teacher, please give it peace."
> Bodhidharma replied, "Bring that mind to me, and I will give it peace."
> "I have searched for the mind, and I cannot find it."
> "There, I have completely set it at rest for you."[6]

This koan again deals with a matter of ultimate concern (as every single one does), which is the realization of that true peace of mind that comes with the resolution of the basic problems of life and death. A surface reading may give the impression that it all happens in one encounter and one exchange of parries and thrusts between the two protagonists. But experience in Zen practice would make it clear that the reply of the Second Ancestor when he confesses, "I have searched for the mind, and I cannot find it," indicates that he has gone through the tedious effort of leg folding and breathing and quieting of the mind for some undetermined amount of time, perhaps for several years, before having reached this answer.

So we must place an extended time frame between Bodhidharma's parry and the Second Ancestor's reply. Bodhidharma's concluding response is an affirmation of the Second Ancestor's realization of true peace of mind, which that indefatigable practice in the extended time frame between the first parry and the reply paved the way for.

The reader may be at a loss at this point, asking, "What in heaven's name is going on here? Didn't the disciple just say, 'I cannot find it,' and now, how can Bodhidharma pat him and say, 'There, I have completely set it at rest for you.'" But the reader must be assured that this is no mere wordplay, but an invitation to an experience. The apparent gap between the disciple's "I cannot find it," and Bodhidharma's "There, I have completely set it at rest for you," is precisely what each practitioner must fill in for oneself, and put oneself totally and wholeheartedly into one's practice, as a matter of life and death. As one does so, one reaches that exact point where "I cannot find it" and "There, I have completely set it at rest for you" converge. Here there is no longer any space in between these two utterances, not even an idea or concept: one arrives at a pure experience of "zero point."

In the same way, the novice monk's reply in our earlier koan, "Yes, I have," presupposes this indefatigable practice before one is able to make such a response, the length of time varying with each individual practitioner. In the context of such wholehearted practice giving one's whole being to a matter of life and death, as one ripens in this practice, one arrives at that moment, or better, that moment arrives in one. This is the actual experience of that fullness of "having had one's meal," in a way that one will no longer go hungry for all eternity. This is a veritable experience of that deep inner peace, the peace that no one can take away. This is likewise the experience of drinking of that living water that Jesus promised to the woman of Samaria whom he met by the well: drinking of this water of eternal life, one will no longer thirst (Jn. 4:14).

Having had one's breakfast, the next and more crucial facet of the Zen life follows, which will engage the practitioner in a lifelong task. Arriving at this stage, one is truly ready to begin.[7]

WASHING ONE'S BOWLS

As one perseveres in the struggle with aching legs and stray thoughts and other things that come up in sitting practice, in due time one is able to get an exquisite taste of what Zen has to offer. For such a person the natural thing would be to want to tell everybody else to try and see how good it is, and to encourage everyone to the same practice.

After an initial phase of struggle and adjustment to the basic elements of practice, there comes a stage of enhanced fervor, as one actually begins to feel the wholesome effects of sitting practice in one's daily life. This, of course, is an expected development, and with this, one is invited to a further and further deepening in one's practice, as the various elements in one's life fall into place in its light.

As one's practice ripens, that pivotal experience of seeing into one's true nature, described earlier as an arrival at "zero-point" but more properly the simple coming-to-the-fore of that which has always been there from the start, can happen anytime. It can be triggered by anything at all under the sun, such as the sight of a flower or a look at a beautiful landscape, the sound of a bird chirping or of someone sneezing or of a baby crying, the touch of another's hand. But in whatever way it comes or one comes to it, such an experience is indeed Earth-shaking, and it can lead to an emotional outburst, totally exhilarating, accompanied by laughter, tears, even convulsions. For some it may not be that exhuberant an expression, but it is basically an experience accompanied by deep inner peace and a quiet and liberating joy, sheer joy at "having come to one's own."

This is a powerful experience that can be totally transformative of one's whole life. In its power, it is quite easy to become attached to that experience, to keep falling back to it instead of moving on to the next step. Or one can pin it on one's lapel, so to speak, and count it among one's possessions, turning it into a cocktail party conversation piece. It is to such persons that Chao-chou's advice is directed: "Wash your bowls!"

Yamada Roshi kept repeating in his Zen talks, as a word of caution to those whose experience he himself had confirmed as genuine Zen enlightenment, that such an experience is comparable to joining the first-grade class in elementary school. It is only really the first step in a lifelong, or better, an infinitely long process that leads one deeper and deeper into the mystery of what life is all about. Of course it is easy for one who has just entered the first grade to be proud of being there, but that would be an entirely misplaced kind of pride. Such misplaced pride, coupled with an inordinate zeal to talk about Zen and its accoutrements, even to those who have least desire for it and in situations out of context with such talk, is aptly termed "Zen sickness." This ailment can range from relatively mild to mortally grave, and is easy to spot at a group meeting (or a cocktail party).

"Wash your bowls."

With a breakfast of nice soft oatmeal, we are ready to face the day, filled, fulfilled, and grateful to be alive. But it is quite easy to forget to wash our bowls, to let the oatmeal dry up and produce a stink. Such is the image frequently repeated by Susan Jion Postal, a Zen priest who leads a group in Rye, New York, to caution those who come to Zen as another kind of spiritual trip. For such persons, practicing Zen is placing another feather in one's cap, lining up another spiritual treasure to add to their collection that may include yoga, macrobiotics, astrology, and so on.[8] Such things, she says, easily stink like old oatmeal.

Indeed, those of us who have begun to lead a life that we may appropriately term as relating to the spiritual are most susceptible to this temptation to let our old oatmeal stick in our bowls and, without our realizing it, let it begin to stink around us.

In this connection, Chogyam Trungpa, a Tibetan Buddhist who was well known in the United States, also cautions us against what he called "spiritual materialism," which can be a subtle form of self-deception with good intentions around it.[9]

Along the same vein, St. John of the Cross names spiritual avarice as one of the factors that bog one down in the dark night of the soul.[10]

Such an attachment to "spiritual goods" can indeed be damaging in many subtle ways that the seeker is least disposed to recognize. One manifestation of this kind of tendency is the attachment to one's spiritual director or teacher. The director or teacher may have helped one on the path, and precisely because of this kind of spiritual relationship, one's attachment to such a person can also develop in an inordinate way and hamper the practitioner's spiritual freedom.[11]

Thus, the continuation of sitting practice, especially after the initial taste of that zero-point mentioned above, is quite crucial in purifying one of such attachments and enabling one to ripen into the wholesome and simple life that Zen is all about. Koan practice after the initial experience of awakening is meant to polish off the sheen that may have accompanied such an experience and enable the practitioner to come back to one's daily life as a normal human being, like any other. As everybody else, one continues life, getting up in the morning, taking one's breakfast, washing up, going to work, getting tired, relaxing, laughing, crying, and so on. But now one is no longer deluded by false ideas of the self and no longer needs to aggrandize that false self beyond proportion.

In short, one is now able to live life in its ordinariness, replete with a sense of its wonder and mystery at every turn. Having seen through the empty nature of that self (i.e., in the light of zero-point), one is also able to realize how that true self is interconnected with everything else in this universe and how everything is connected with that true self, which, more properly speaking, is a no-self.

This realization of interconnectedness is the basis for the natural flowering of a life of com-passion, that is, suffering-with all beings in the universe that one no longer sees as separate from oneself.

"Washing our bowls" is a continual process that we are invited to undertake, day by day, moment to moment. It is a stance of not clinging to anything at all, not even to our spiritual possessions, continuing to let go and be open to the newness of every moment with every breath we are given. Such a stance will keep our eyes open to the miracle of the ordinary right before us every moment of our lives. Washing one's bowls in Zen is to live every moment in its freshness, in celebration of its mystery.

TO BECOME AS LITTLE CHILDREN

The continual stance of "washing our bowls" polishes our inner eye to be able to see the miracle that is right in our very ordinariness.

In Zen talks I sometimes refer to the story someone told me

in Japan about a young father and his little three-year-old daughter, taking a Sunday stroll hand in hand through a meadow one day in spring. They came upon a particular clearing where there were clusters of violets, and the little girl broke loose from the father's hand and began to prance about, dancing among the flowers. "Look, Daddy, look!"

The father was, of course, watching with quiet pride, and with a knowing air, said, "Yes, dear, those are violets." The little girl just continued dancing and prancing, uttering the new word: "Violets! Violets!"

One does not need to go to lengths to explain the point here, which is the difference between the modes of awareness of the little girl and her father. The little girl, wide-eyed and full of wonder at everything around her, saw the flowers in their pristine beauty before she could name what they were. This beauty right before her simply moved her to dance and prance about in joy and celebration of be-ing, be-ing with, unsullied by any dualistic thought or frame of mind. It is an awareness of be-ing filled with mystery and wonder at beholding the simple beauty of nature.

The father, on the other hand, having come to adulthood and now wise in the ways of the world, "knew" what those flowers were over there — violets — and in so knowing, lost the ability to see them in their freshness and mystery of their be-ing. "Those are violets." The human capacity to name things, giving us a certain sense of being in control over the things we can name, takes its toll upon our mode of awareness, and we lose that sense of mystery and wonder that anything is there at all in the first place.

"Why are there existing things rather than nothing?" Martin Heidegger posed this question in the very first line of his book *Introduction to Metaphysics*.[12] Such a question does not demand a verbal answer that will satisfy the questioner, but simply evokes a quality of awareness in us, that throws light on our very mode of be-ing. Our very mode of be-ing is that which necessarily has to raise such a question of "Why are there things rather than nothing?"

To fail to raise such a question, either by letting it be buried in the multitude of mundane concerns that face us in day-today life or simply forgetting it in our preoccupation with getting ahead or making a profit or making a name for oneself, is to become less than what we really are as human beings. The malady of Western civilization, ventured Heidegger, is "the forgetfulness of Be-ing." Getting lost in the business of securing our livelihood, we lose our life in the process.

Asking the question, "Why are there things rather than nothing?" is one form of giving expression to the awareness of the mystery that we are, to the mystery that the universe is. The question is not to be quenched by an answer such as "because such and such is the case, therefore . . . there are things, and not nothing." Neither is it solved by giving a traditional religious formula such as "God made all things out of nothing." Any child will immediately counter, "Who made God, then?" Such a traditional formula, "God made all things out of nothing," responds to the issue in the same way as the father's utterance to the little daughter dancing with the violets, that is, in a way that takes away the sense of mystery and replaces it with a readymade explanation.

But we have already lost our innocence. The process by which we learn how to live as a human being in this world, which we call "education," and through which we are taught how to name more and more things, leads us into thinking that we can attain mastery of everything in the universe. The deeper we get into the process, the higher the "education" we receive, the farther away from this sense of wonder and mystery we are taken.

Unfortunately, having learned to name things and thus base our self-understanding on this separation and distinction from everything we can name, we become acutely aware of being isolated, alienated in this universe. "I" am here, and everything else (including other human beings) stands out there as object to me.

This is the frame of mind that has led to our human desire to have control over things as well as other people, and nature as well, since we are laden with a deep anxiety at our separateness from them. We can say that it is out of a deep longing to reconnect, to overcome this sense of separateness, which makes us feel alienated and insecure, that the desire to control, to have power over things, over other people, over nature as a whole, somehow takes sway in us. But it is an entirely misplaced way of trying to overcome that sense of separateness, as we only manage to deepen the gulf in the attempt. With our attempts at achieving greater mastery and control over things around us, we only succeed in deepening the woundedness at the core of our being.

The very desire to know, in the sense of the knowledge of objects in the universe, comes from the same deep longing to reconnect. I become insecure, even threatened, by not knowing about something out there, and so I pursue what Aristotle called the natural human desire to know. This is the same sense by which Francis Bacon, at the beginning of the so-called Modern Age of human history, proclaimed that "knowledge is power."

It is that dubious power that comes out of that kind of objective knowledge that has led us to where we are today as Earth community. We are now at the brink of destruction by that very power that we have sought to control nature, as well as the lives of people, using the highly advanced kinds of knowledge that we have acquired for ourselves.

We have exercised what we have understood to be our God-given prerogative to name things in this universe, and in so doing, have lost the sense of mystery and *God-givenness* of all these. Our advance in knowledge, with its corollary increase in our power over nature, has caused us to desacralize everything in the universe and regard everything as mere objects to be placed under our control or to be used for our purposes. We have lost that sense of wonder, the sense of the sacredness of the flowers, in being able to name them as "violets."

Having lost that original innocence and original sense of wonder, there is no way for us to go back to this pristine state. We have learned to name things around us, as a prerogative and distinctive trait of our human condition, there is no escaping from this anymore. Our salvation can no longer be sought in a simple return to a pristine state before we "knew" and "ate of the fruit of the tree of knowledge of good and evil."

The question is, is there salvation for us, having eaten of that fruit?

The dancing little girl again deserves our look.

Learning how to name those beautiful things around her from

her father, she exclaims, "Violets! Violets!" And she continued dancing.

Having learned to name the flowers did not necessarily take away the sense of mystery and wonder and beauty that was there to be celebrated. Her knowing what to call them did not make her lose the awareness of the mystery that they were. The dance, in fact, attained a new quality in that she could now properly address those she was dancing with: "Violets! Violets!"

The dancing little girl shows us that perhaps there is a way for us who have lost our innocence, who have known separation, in having learned the ways of the world, to still recover the sense of mystery and learn again how to dance with the violets. Morris Berman called this, in a book that made some ripples when it came out some years ago, the need for "the reenchantment of the world."[13]

We have learned the name of the violets, but that does not mean we have any power over them. "Even Solomon, in all his glory, was not arrayed like one of these" (Mt. 6:29), we are reminded by the Bible. We may have succeeded in conducting experiments to affect the genes of plants and animals and even human beings, to alter their form in ways more suited to our human intentions and purposes, but it is not, and never will be, in our power to call violets into being.

What is in our power is to cause them to cease to be, as we are causing thousands of species to cease to be, with the way we live and relate to Earth. One cannot but shudder at this kind of so-called power we have acquired, all rooted in that sense of separateness and the misplaced way of trying to overcome it. Our deep-seated longing to reconnect with nature, with other people, with the universe, needs to be redirected to its original course. In other words, we are called to learn once again to dance with the violets.

"Unless you become as these little children, you shall not enter the reign of God" (Mt. 18:3). Jesus' words invite us to a recovery of a mode of being, to a mode of awareness that will heal our cosmic woundedness.

THE WONDER OF A CUP OF TEA

There is an apocryphal story of an International Meditators' Convention where people adept in the meditative practice of their respective traditions were invited to present the best of what their tradition had to offer. The finalists were narrowed down to three, the first two from traditions which will remain unnamed here, and the third a Zen monk from Japan.

The first of the finalists took the stage, went into a trance, and within minutes could be seen to be levitating six inches above the floor, cushion and all! Within minutes, this adept settled back on the stage floor, was out of the trance, stood up, and bowed to the standing ovation of the audience. The second finalist was called in, took the cushion, and likewise within minutes went into deep meditation. Then an assistant appeared and let out a swarm of gigantic mosquitoes from a bottle. The mosquitoes swooped upon the second finalist and began biting from every angle they could find, but the adept was not moved, remaining in meditation until the mosquitoes grew tired, finding their way out of the arena. Again, a standing ovation as the second finalist awoke from the trance refreshed, without as much as a mark from a mosquito bite.

The third finalist, the Zen monk from Japan, was called in, and bowing several times, first to the assistants on the stage and then to the audience, took a seat on the round cushion at the center of the stage. Assuming a cross-legged posture, breathing normally yet deeply, the monk sat quietly in Zen meditation. Everyone was in silence all through this time, as if partaking in the inner peace and silence of the meditator, all eyes focused on the center of the stage where the monk sat. Then, as twenty-five minutes went by, an assistant rang a bell, the monk joined his palms in a gesture of reverence and made a bow to the audience. The assistant then came in with a cup of tea on a tray and offered it to the monk, who again bowed in gratitude and sipped the tea, smiling at the audience, saying, "Ah, delicious. Thank you very much."

The audience was at full attention, still waiting for something spectacular to happen, as with the two previous contestants. But the Zen monk simply had another serving, returned the cup, and, again giving thanks, bowed and left the stage. The audience remained in silence for a while, until one by one they began to nod in recognition, and then smiling, nod to one another, enwrapped by a peaceful and reassuring sense of having rediscovered something very precious.

It took time for the audience to realize what had come over them: the deep sense of satisfaction at having glimpsed something of the grand fruit of the Zen life, which the monk embodied in his simple presence. Sitting quietly, taking one's tea, being grateful, taking one's exit—that is all. No fireworks or spectacular displays, just opening one's eyes to the miracle of it all—the wonder of a cup of tea.

The above story is, of course, exaggerated and apocryphal, concocted evidently by someone from within or sympathetic to the Zen tradition, but the point is brought home. Zen is not for those who are expecting some kind of spectacular result from meditation, such as levitation or the attainment of superhuman psychic powers. Of course, these are not precluded, if they come as a natural and unsought fruit of long years of practice, but they are not what Zen is about. The best that Zen has to offer cannot be fathomed by those who look to it for some ulterior motive.

Even what is often talked about as kensho, or the experience of enlightenment, is not to be considered a goal to be sought after and attained through one's own effort. It is a kind of experience that can be totally transformative, and is of course what draws people to Zen practice. But if it is regarded as some kind of thing that is good to have, some goodie consumer item or scout merit badge that would be great to possess and pin on to one's lapel, then one becomes sidetracked and misses the whole point.

What Zen offers is an invitation to "taste and see," the quiet joy of simply be-ing, of sitting, of standing, walking, laughing, crying. Getting up in the middle of the night to soothe a crying baby back to sleep. Waking up in the morning, washing one's face. Going to work, coming home. Playing with the children. Listening to music. Putting out the garbage. Sorting out plastics and bottles for recycling. Writing a letter to one's senator. Joining a picket line. Lining up in a soup kitchen. Getting tired. Growing old. Battling with cancer. Dying of AIDS. *Just that.* And in the midst of all this, to experience a miracle.

To embody the way of the awakened in our daily life is *just that*—nothing more than living every moment, just as it is, emptied of ego, filled with a sense of mystery and wonder.

I am reminded of an incident in my mid-teens, when I was on my way to an open-air dance party in my hometown in the Philippines. I happened to be walking side-by-side with a friend we shall call Al, who was in first year medical school at the time. My heart was already thumping with expectation at nearing the plaza where the dance was to be held, but as we were walking along the way, Al began to tell me of the anatomy class they had the day before.

He began to relate how they dissected a human cadaver and how they opened the torso and examined the lungs, the heart, the liver, the other internal organs, as the instructor explained their functions and their interrelations. But what Al wanted to share with me was the profound impression all this left upon him—how the human body was structured in such a delicate and marvelous way that we humans have never been and can never be able to completely figure out. And how he could only exclaim, in awe and wonder, "Unthinkable, that all this could be out of mere chance!"

He pointed out how something like a radio or a television set could only be put together and function by applying the best that human genius could offer in finding out the laws of electricity and figuring out the various interconnections of the elements that, put together, are able to transmit signals sent from afar through this tiny electronic box. He also conveyed his realization of how he was face-to-face with something infinitely more complex than a radio or television set. "Unthinkable, that all this could be out of mere chance."

Al's sharing somehow touched a deep chord within me, and I recall sensing the thumping of my heart in excitement with a new awareness—the awareness of mystery expressed in Al's "Unthinkable, that all this could be out of mere chance." We finally reached the plaza, joined the dance, and the open-air dance party went on. But for me that evening the band played a different kind of music, and the stars above showed a different kind of glow. "Unthinkable . . . all this . . . mere chance."[14]

Again, it was not a matter of simply concluding that "Therefore, there is a God" and thereby settling the issue. This, of course, was one way I could express it at that time. Based on the religious conceptual framework of my traditional Roman

Catholic upbringing, the term "God" came to take on a new level of meaning for me. But it was not so much a question of holding on to a notion or definition of the term "God," as one of sensing deep within oneself that "there is an unfathomable Wisdom in all this," that there is point in the existence of the universe, and that, ultimately, *we are in good hands.*

That sense of "unthinkable . . . " remained with me and came to be more clear and distinct as I was led further into Zen. With Zen practice, one grows into an awareness that every heartbeat, every breath, or even every hair on my head, as well as every newborn baby, every blade of grass, every pebble by the wayside, is something "unthinkable," something that calls forth a sense of wonder on every count: a veritable miracle.

It is the recovery of this sense of wonder and mystery of everything that can heal the rift I find between myself and nature, between myself and my fellow humans. As I live every moment replete with this sense of wonder and mystery, such a mode of awareness encompasses the whole of nature, all human beings, as well as my own self, and grounds the vivid sense of my connectedness with everything in the universe.

6.

This Is My Body

Zen practice, with the attention given to posture, breathing, and the focusing of one's whole being on the here and now in the following of the breath, makes one more deeply sensitive to the continuing miracle that is this very body. In this chapter we will explore the dimensions opened to us in "this very body" in the light of Zen practice. The hope is that in so doing we may be able to see its cosmic implications and get a glimpse of its "breadth and length and height and depth" (Eph. 3:18), and we may thereby recover the sense of its sacredness, but also find the way to the healing of its brokenness.

DROPPING OFF BODY AND MIND

In the closing lines of Zen master Hakuin's (1686-1769) famous Song of Zazen, which is chanted in Zen temples all over Japan and translated into other languages and chanted in Zen halls all over the world, we encounter the reference to "this very body" in the final refrain:

> At this moment, what is it you seek?
> Nirvana is right here before you.
> Lotus Land is right here.
> This very body, the body of the Buddha.[1]

This Song of Zazen, which expresses in a beautiful and poetic way the heart of Zen enlightenment, conveys a powerful message: "Do not look outside of yourself, no need to look afar: what you seek is right here, right where you are."[2]

The core of Zen practice consists in focusing our whole being, in all that it involves, in the here and now, in following our breath. Those of us who have begun to take up the invitation to this practice, even for a little while, realize it is not as simple a thing as it sounds placing our whole being in the here and now. This is because our whole being is not fully there, dispersed as we are in different directions, the various elements often at odds and in opposition with one another.

The most basic opposition we encounter in ourselves is that apparent between "body" and "mind." Our body is right here, sitting in lotus or half-lotus position or in some modified version, and if we are slack in our practice, within a few minutes our mind has begun to wander in another dimension or in pursuit of a stray thought that takes us to a past experience, an anticipated event, or something happening or not happening elsewhere.

Zazen invites us to experience the body and mind not in this separated and oppositional kind of way, but as an organic and dynamic unity. It invites us to let our mind be fully here and now, right here in full awareness as I sit with my back straight and my legs folded and my whole body in a relaxed but attentive posture, right now in full awareness of time, time seen not as a linear flux of a series of present moments receding into the past, but as an ever-present *now* experienced in each breath.

As we deepen in this practice, we are enabled to glimpse that world of nonopposition of our body-mind; the world where, in the words of Zen master Dogen, the body and mind "drop off."

> To learn the way of the awakened is to learn
>   the self.
> To learn the self is to forget the self.
> To forget the self is to perceive the self in all
>   things.
> To perceive the self in all things is to drop off
>   one's own body-mind as well as to drop

off the other's body-mind.

> As one reaches this, there is no more trace of
> enlightenment, but one simply lives this
> enlightenment-without-a-trace.[3]

"Dropping off body-mind" is an expression which, according to written accounts, triggered Dogen's own experience of enlightenment, which he presented to and had recognized by his teacher, Ju-ching, while he was in China.

Let us examine a little more closely the phrases in this short account of the way of the Awakened given by Dogen to provide us with a clue into this dimension that he is inviting us to experience for ourselves.

First, this way of the Awakened is no other than the way of realization of one's true self. That true self, however, is not to be conceived of as a substance or entity that is out there or even in here, waiting to be discovered, but as something that is realized precisely in forgetting it altogether. Forgetting the self in this way breaks the imagined wall between the self and all things in the universe, that is, the wall we tend to place between our self and the Other.

This is "dropping off one's own body-mind," which is also "dropping off the *other's* body-mind," in Dogen's account. What remains? Not a single trace of enlightenment, as a self-conscious attitude and mental framework, but simply a raw actualization of every concrete event in our daily life, as we get up in the morning, take breakfast, go to work, take a rest, stand up, sit down, laugh, cry.

So "this very body, the body of the Buddha" (the Awakened One) referred to in Hakuin's Song of Zazen does not, or ought not, let us take off into a kind of speculation or intellectual leap that would equate or identify "this very body" with some metaphysically conceived "body of the Buddha" out there, and lead us to make a presumptuous statement such as "my body is the Buddha-body." Nothing could be further from true awakening than this, which is a mere bloating up of one's delusive self that one misleadingly identifies with Buddha.

No, true awakening, Dogen reminds us, is "dropping off body-mind," which is actualized in forgetting of one's self. We are invited to enter into a paradox here: to forget one's self, and in that very forgetfulness of self, to realize the way of the Awakened. "This very body, the body of the Buddha," in the very mundane, yet wondrous events of breathing, standing, sitting, walking, laughing, crying.

In more technical language, this is a direct mode of awareness that breaks through the subject-object barrier created by our ego-centered consciousness.

This ego-centered consciousness tends to assume that the self is a subject in here or within, looking out and perceiving objects that are without. In this ego-consciousness based on the distinction of subject and object, we separate our self from the Other, but also tend to look even at our body as an object that is perceived by the conscious self or the "I." In this framework I "have" my body; I control it and move it this way or that way as I will. This is the way the Western philosophical tradition, especially since Descartes, has presented a common-sense understanding of the structure of the self vis-à-vis the world, i.e., everything else that stands in opposition to this self.

Such a way of understanding the self in basic opposition to my body and to the rest of the world, to God, has dominated the Western worldview for so long now and has been the underlying presupposition in our presumptuous attempts to conquer and control nature as part of that which is out there as an object. We come to realize the fallacy as well as the self-destructive effects of such a way of conceiving the self in the context of a subject-object dichotomy. Based on this conception, we have come to an acute sense of our alienation from nature, from our body, and from our own deepest self.

In recent decades, developments in phenomenology and philosophy, as well as in theology, have opened the way in the West for the retrieval of the awareness of the body not as something that "I have," but as a lived body which "I am."[4] Eastern traditions, on the other hand, have been less prone to see things in terms of a dichotomy, and this mode of awareness of the lived body as the locus of true selfhood has been transmitted since time immemorial.[5]

Zen practice offers a direct way that enables us to overcome this way of understanding the self in opposition to our body, in inviting us to sit still and experience our body-mind in dynamic unity in every here and now. As we do so, we are opened to the experience Dogen refers to, that of "dropping off one's body-mind and dropping off the other's body-mind," and the door is opened to an entirely new way of be-ing, to a new perspective of seeing the self in all things and all things as the self. Let us go on to unpack this some more.

THIS VERY BODY, THE GREAT WIDE EARTH

Let us look further at what is implied by this new way of being alluded to above, helped by an account of the enlightenment experience of my own Zen teacher, Yamada Koun Roshi, written when he was still in his forties. Here let me present an extended excerpt from his account, included in Philip Kapleau's *Three Pillars of Zen*.[6]

Yamada relates the experience that occurred as he was reading a book while on a train with his wife from Tokyo on the way home to Kamakura.

As the train was nearing Ofuna station I ran across this line: "I came to realize clearly that Mind is no other than mountains and rivers and the great wide earth, the sun and the moon and the stars."

I had read this before, but this time it impressed itself upon me so vividly that I was startled. I said to myself: "after seven or eight years of zazen I have finally perceived the essence of this statement," and couldn't suppress the tears that began to well up. Somewhat ashamed to find myself crying among the crowd, I averted my face and dabbed at my eyes with my handkerchief.

Meanwhile the train had arrived at Kamakura station and my wife and I got off. On the way home I said to her: "In my present exhilarated frame of mind I could rise to the greatest heights." Laughingly, she replied, "Then where would I be?" All the while I kept repeating the quotation to myself.

(That night) . . . it was after eleven thirty that I went to bed. At midnight I abruptly awakened. At first my mind was foggy, then suddenly that quotation flashed into my consciousness: "I came to realize clearly that Mind is no other than mountains, rivers, and the great wide earth, the sun and the moon and the stars." And I repeated it. Then all at once I was struck as though by lightning, and the next instant heaven and earth crumbled and disappeared.

Instantaneously, like surging waves, a tremendous delight welled up in me, a veritable hurricane of delight, as I laughed loudly and widely, "Ha, ha, ha, ha, ha, ha! There's no reasoning here, no reasoning at all! Ha, ha, ha!"

The empty sky split in two, then opened its enormous mouth and began to laugh uproariously: "Ha, ha, ha!"

Although twenty-four hours have elapsed, I still feel the aftermath of that earthquake. My entire body is still shaking. I spent all of today laughing and weeping by myself.

The above passage is presented as an account of a powerful experience that transformed one individual person, who in turn came to be a significant presence that led to the transformation of many other persons who came into contact with him or received his personal guidance in their Zen practice.

What we would like to examine at this point is what triggered the experience, namely, the short passage from a work of Zen master Dogen that literally leapt out as he was reading his book: "I came to realize clearly that Mind is no other than mountains and rivers and the great wide earth, the sun and the moon and the stars."[7]

Our task here is not so much to present an analysis of this passage, as if by such an analysis one could fully elucidate its implications and automatically lead the reader to the same experience of enlightenment. Such an attempt would only be like scratching an itching foot on top of one's leather shoe. Pursuing this analogy, the practice of Zen would be the endeavor to take off that shoe that blocks access to the itching foot: this is casting away that subject-object mode of approaching things with our ego-centered consciousness and baring our naked self in the process. This ego-centered consciousness tends to make us assume that "I" am here and that mind is the activity of the "I," making use of the senses, to see, hear, smell, taste, touch, or imagine things out there such as mountains, rivers, the sun, the moon, stars.

In this same framework, my body is seen no less as an object vis-à-vis the mind, although more in here than out there. Ego-centered consciousness is built upon these oppositions of mind vs. body, as well as mind vs. things out there (mountains, rivers, trees).

In the practice of zazen, one is enjoined to set the mind in stillness, letting it be fully absorbed in the here and now in following every breath. As one deepens in this practice, one's being simply ripens in awareness, and one becomes ready for the moment when all those oppositions taken for granted in ego-centered consciousness disintegrate. Literally, one's body-mind drops off, and the Other's body-mind drops off. What is left?

This can be likened to the process of peeling an onion. One simply peels away one layer after another, and eventually, in a tearful moment, one reaches the core of the onion. What is left?

This is the moment of realization of one's true self, which is in reality no-self. This no-self is described in Buddhist texts by a series of negations, such as we see in the famous *Heart Sutra**, which is frequently recited in Zen temples all over the world: "no form, no sound, no odor, no taste, no object of touch, no image."

In a previous work I referred to this moment as the arrival at zero-point, that point where all opposites merge, where all the positive and negative elements in our being, as well as in the whole universe, merge, and in so merging, become fully transformed.[8]

It is this arrival at zero-point that enables one to place oneself at the fulcrum upon which the whole universe hangs. From this zero-point, one is able to move the world at will and "walk freely in the universe," as Wu Men, the compiler of the famous collection of koans called *Wu Men Kuan*, wrote in his poem introducing the collection.[9]

It is from the perspective of this zero-point that the following exchange between two Zen monks takes place:

Officer Lu Geng said to Nanquan, "Teaching Master Zhao was quite extraordinary: he was able to say, 'Heaven and earth have the same root, myriad things are one body.' "

Nanquan pointed to a peony in the garden, and said, "People today see this flower as in a dream."[10]

In our ego-centered consciousness, where we separate the self as subject from objects outside, we are not able to see things as they truly are, but only as perceived from that self thought to be within. The philosopher Immanuel Kant noted how we can only see "things as they appear" (phenomena) and will never be able to grasp "things as they are" (noumena) in our subject-object mode of perception. Thus, as Nanquan points out in the above dialogue, those who are not able to overcome this subject-object polarity in ordinary ego-centered consciousness can only "see this flower as in a dream"; that is, they do not see it as it really is.

As one arrives at and sees things from zero-point, one can say with teaching master Zhao, "Heaven and earth have the same root, myriad things are one body." "Myriad things" here refers to each and every particular thing in the entire universe: mountains, rivers, the sun and moon and stars, this chair, that table, the coffee cup.

From this perspective of zero-point, one is also able to exclaim with Hakuin in the Song of Zazen, "this very body, the body of the Buddha (= the Awakened)," not as a statement on a metaphysical plane, but as a pointer to the dimensions opened with the experience of awakening. Again from this perspective, "this very body" is no longer merely "this physical body of mine," which I tend to place in opposition to the physical bodies of others, and thus also still in opposition to all other myriad things in the universe. As my mind's eye is opened, "this very body" is no longer something different from mountains and rivers, the sun and moon and stars.

HOLOGRAM: THE PART IS THE WHOLE

What I have just described concerning the Zen enlightenment experience, that arrival at zero-point that enables one to exclaim that "heaven and earth have the same root, myriad things are one body," can be approached from a different angle.

I was made aware of a fascinating dimension of our bodiliness as I went back for a family visit to the Philippines some years ago and had the opportunity to have a talk with my youngest brother, who is a medical doctor teaching at a university. He related to me his dilemmas in practicing medicine in a semi-rural, semi-urban area in the Philippines, where he originally opened a clinic. The majority of those who came to him had hardly enough money to pay for his services, let alone the funds to buy the kind of medicine he was taught by his Western-oriented medical training to prescribe for their treatment, and so it broke his heart to charge them just enough to meet his own and his family's upkeep. This led him to explore different ways of healing, and thus he began his studies in Oriental medicine.

After a while he became proficient in acupuncture and had begun to attract patients looking for this kind of treatment for various kinds of ailments. With this he felt that the treatment did not have to require a great amount of money to buy expensive drugs, especially on the part of his poorer patients. But he also related how he had a growing clientele of financially well-to-do persons who wanted acupuncture treatment to help them lose weight. He told me that if one applies an acupuncture needle at a certain place in a person's earlobes, the person would lose the appetite for certain rich foods. The overall effect would be a general loss of weight within two weeks. If one continued the acupuncture treatment, they could lose as much as ten to twenty pounds. He was beginning a lucrative practice for such persons, and the remuneration from this would balance off what he did not charge from his less-well-to-do patients with more basic ailments.

This story of my brother's acupuncture practice opened my eyes anew to the fascinating world of the human body that the Chinese had discovered and had been putting into practical use for thousands of years. Different parts of our body interconnect with one another, and the proper stimulation of certain parts inevitably brings about a healing effect on other parts. The ear, for example, is something like a minuscule model of the whole body, with each part (of the ear) corresponding to some other part of the bigger whole. This discovery was the basis of the application for healing the whole body, and the fascinating thing about it was that it worked!

This account of my brother is corroborated by what I learned from an Indonesian Jesuit I met while attending a conference near Jogyakarta. During one meeting I noticed a slight headache due to sinus problems. I mentioned this during break to the above Jesuit, who was helping us with odds and ends for the conference, and he motioned me aside and asked me to sit down and take off my shoes. Having done so, he proceeded to massage my toes and certain areas of the soles of my feet, one after the other. Within minutes, I felt relief from my headache and from the discomfort of my sinus condition.

While he was massaging my feet, he explained to me how the various areas of the foot correspond to different parts of the body, and massaging those areas led to relief from certain ailments in the kidneys, bladder, stomach, lungs, and other internal organs that correspond to the areas being massaged. The same thing could be done, hc said, to the palms of the hands, as they also have similar correspondences.

This same person told me of how he had given basic instructions on this way of healing to another priest who was visiting their seminary, a German-born Jesuit who was teaching Hebrew Scriptures and Rabbinical Literature at the Gregorian University in Rome. This Jesuit was on his way to spend a sabbatical year helping out at a relief agency for refugees in Africa. He later gave a report on his experiences with the people he worked with in Africa and related how he applied what he learned of this way of healing. He recounted his astonishment at the results of the simple foot massages he had performed on so many persons who came to him for healing of their different ailments.

The above accounts brought home to me an added element of wonder at our human bodiliness. The ear, the soles of the feet, the palms of the hand, in a very concrete and tangible kind of way, all contain in themselves the whole body, with corresponding parts placed in isomorphic fashion. The Western scientific mind may remain skeptical about these, but recent discoveries regarding holistic healing and reflexology, now being treated in books available in Western languages, corroborate these accounts.

Let me mention an example to illustrate our point: the work of Karl Pribram, a neuroscientist at Stanford, whose research into the human brain has led to some startling perspectives, and has come to be seen in connection with and as complementing the work of physicist David Bohm.

Without going into detail, we can simply summarize these new vistas being opened in the scientific world with the word "hologram." This is a term taken from lensless photography to indicate an image whose every part can be enlarged and shown to contain the whole. For example, if we have a holographic picture of a mountain, and we cut one section of it, this section will, upon enlargement, show not just the part cut out (such as the foot, or one side, or the tip), but the whole mountain. The same process could be repeated with the new image, with the same results. In short, each part contains the whole, completely and without deficiency.

It may be difficult to imagine, but this has been the constant result of repeated photographic experiments with this kind of image, which is produced by recording the wave field of light scattered by an object on a plate. When this record of one wave field is placed in a coherent light beam (such as a laser), the original wave pattern is reproduced, and we see a whole three-dimensional image, exactly like the original pattern. In other words, any part of the image will reproduce the whole.

The work of Karl Pribram and David Bohm in neurobiology and physics, respectively, points to an understanding of the human brain—and of the whole universe—as a hologram. In short, each part of our brain and each part of this universe contains the whole.[11]

For many of us, these are startling statements, indeed, difficult to fathom from our ordinary "common sense" consciousness that separates the perceiving subject from the whole universe of objects and sees these objects as set against one another. They are statements that invite us to place ourselves at a different vantage point when looking at things, at a different fulcrum that enables us to see the whole picture.

Yet such a perspective is not a novel one at all, but one that has been opened to those who arrived at zero-point, through various ways of meditative practice, since time immemorial. Ancient Hindu texts, as well as Buddhist texts, are full of descriptions that issue forth from this matrix of zero-point.

The Jewel Net of Indra, an interconnected net wherein each jewel fully reflects all the others, is one such image frequently referred to in bringing out this point. In China this came to be developed and expounded in Hua Yen philosophy, by a Buddhist philosophical school deriving inspiration from a sutra of the same name.[12]

Surprisingly enough, we can also find this same imagery in a basic notion in traditional Christianity: the notion of the Mystical Body.

THE MYSTICAL BODY OF CHRIST

The description of the universe as a hologram, wherein every part contains the whole, is the very image given in the traditional Christian doctrine on the eucharistic bread as the Body of Christ.

I recall my catechism teacher explaining to us children that the white round wafer was the real Body of Christ, and that each one was the fullness of the same Christ. We were reassured that whether one received a whole round host or half of a host (for sometimes the priest would divide the remaining hosts so there would be enough to go around), each piece was in itself the full Body of Christ, no less. At that time it was by a simple act of (blind) faith that I was able to accept what the catechism teacher told us about the fullness of Christ in each piece of the eucharistic bread.

In this connection, I also recall an incident at San-un Zendo in Japan, where a Christian member of our Zen community was trying to explain the Eucharist to Yamada Roshi during a gathering over tea after a Zen sitting session. (I must note here that Yamada Roshi had been receiving many Christians as his Zen disciples since the early 1970s, and during Zen retreats he had given permission for the Christians participating in these retreats at his Zen temple to have their own eucharistic celebration in another room while the Buddhists were chanting their morning sutras in the main Zen hall.) This member expressed it in simple terms. "We Christians believe that the bread offered in the Eucharist is the real Body of Christ." Whereupon Yamada Roshi, without the least bit of surprise or doubt, simply replied, "But of course!"

In other words, from his enlightened perspective, he was able to see and understand clearly (much more than many Christians could ever do) the reality of the Divine Presence in the eucharistic bread, as a matter so obvious and plain to the (enlightened) eye.

An enlightened eye is not so much a special or esoteric way of seeing accessible only to a few, but a way of seeing things as they really are, a way that has overcome the subject-object dichotomy that characterizes our ordinary ego-centered consciousness. It is a way of seeing open to all, if only the veil caused by this dualistic habit of mind would be lifted. Zen practice is precisely about the lifting of such a veil, in quieting our dualistic mind and enabling it to rest upon zero-point, so that things will be seen in their true and original light.

In a meditative way, then, let us take the hint from the Christian celebration of the Eucharist, that we may get a glimmer of the new heaven and new earth that it invites us to enter. Let us put ourselves in the context of a eucharistic celebration at this point, and follow the steps it is leading us to.

We can begin by simply placing our gaze on the bread and the wine that are to be offered in the celebration, and taking it from there. First of all, where does this bread come from, and whence the wine? Here we are invited to trace the elements we have right before us to their source. We see the wheat growing in the fields, the grapes dangling from the vines. The wheat and the grapes are connected to the earth through the grain stalk and the vine, respectively, nourished in the bosom of the great wide Earth, with its rich soil full of minerals and natural nutrients, where all sorts of living beings, such as bacteria and earthworms also thrive and contribute their share in the nurturing of life. Rain falling from the clouds waters this great wide Earth, letting its nutrients flow through the roots of the plants. The plants also receive nourishment from the sun, from the energy that strikes the green leaves for the process of photosynthesis, and in the carbon dioxide and other elements needed to continue the nurturing process. In the process, plants return oxygen to the atmosphere, which numerous animal species need for their own life process, in a constant give and take.

The above is just a rough description of the various interconnections we can see in simply gazing at the bread and wine placed before us to be offered in the celebration of thanksgiving we call the Eucharist.

In all this, we can also see the work of countless human hands, who have put in their share in the whole process that brought the wheat and the grapes to this table in the form of bread and wine. The rough hands that tended the soil, as well as the caring hands of their spouses, the little hands of their children. The hands of those who labored in the mills and wine presses and packing factories, the hands of the truck drivers (and those of their families who stayed at home and waited for the return of their bread providers after several days of absence in delivering their truckloads to far-off places), of the retail storekeepers and their employees, struggling to manage on their meager incomes. The fruits of the labor of the whole human community can be seen right here, in this bread and wine prepared for the offering.

The prayer of the community echoes all these sets of interconnections quite pointedly. "Blessed are you, God of all creation. Through Your goodness we have this bread and wine to offer. Fruits of the earth, the work of human hands." So what we have being offered here, in and through this single piece of bread and this one cup of wine, is the whole interconnected network that led to this piece of bread and this cup of wine — the whole of God's creation and the fruits of the labor of the whole human community. It is this totality that we have right here before us, as we prepare for the pronouncement of those sacred words: "this is my body, given for you."

Again, we recall that this offering, being made at this particular point in human history at this particular locale, is not something done as an isolated instance at this linear point in time in this concrete geographical place where we happen to be holding the eucharistic celebration. "Do this in remembrance of me." In other words, it is a re-collection, a re-enactment, a re-living of an event that happened around two thousand years ago some-where in Palestine, when Jesus took the bread, took the cup, and gave it to his disciples, signifying the offering of himself in obedience to the Father, an obedience that would lead him to death on the cross. With that death on the cross there came a newness of life, the life of the Risen Christ that now fills the universe.

This eucharistic celebration that Christians participate in is a re-enactment of that same offering of Christ of his whole being to God, and re-presents a primal event that cuts through all of history and gives it its meaning.

In following this invitation to take up the bread and wine and offer it in thanksgiving to the Source of all creation, we are putting ourselves in a dimension that cuts through all time, "before the foundation of the world" (Eph. 1:4) and across all space, through "all things in heaven and all things on earth" (Eph. 1:10), and comes to participate in a primal event where the meaning of our very be-ing is brought into full light: "This is my body, given for you."

These words then take us through all time and through all space, in the very here and now where we are, and put us in touch with the very foundations of the universe. "This is my body, given for you." This bread and wine, which is no less than the whole of creation and the whole community of living beings in their interconnected way of be-ing right here before us, is offered in thanksgiving to the Source of all creation, in and through the offering of Jesus' whole life, a life lived in total obedience, even to death on the cross.

The utterance of these words, "This is my body, given for you," opens to those "with eyes that see" the very secret of the universe itself, and with this, one is also able to partake in the newness of life that fills all in all, pulsing right here and now.

The bread and wine is not just there to be gazed at, but is there to be consumed by all participants in the eucharistic cel-ebration. As each one receives the elements of the bread and wine, the original words are heard with a more intimate kind of resonance: "This is my body, given for you." As the bread is consumed and dissolves into the communicant's body, one is invited to listen again: "This is my body, given for you."

In other words, each instance of participation in the eucharistic celebration is an invitation to each of us to behold the cosmic dimensions of what is happening right here before us. It is an invitation to cut through our dualistic modes of thinking, to overcome our subject-object duality, and to put ourselves across all time and across all space, to that primal event that throws light on the very meaning of our being, that opens to us the reality of our true self, as we listen to the words, "this is my body, given for you."

The eucharistic celebration can be our passage to mystic depths as we open ourselves to the experience of "this very body" in its cosmic dimensions right before our eyes. At the same time, however, this experience also brings us back down to Earth, in touch with the concrete realities happening to this broken body that is Earth itself.

THE BODY BROKEN

In the Roman Catholic rite, the participating congregation is invited to turn to one another for the greeting of peace just before the reception of communion, while in some Methodist churches I have attended, this greeting of peace is sometimes shared just after communion. Whether offered before or after the reception of the communion bread, this greeting of peace is meant to remind the community that the Body that each one partakes of, though one and undivided at its source from all eternity, is still in a state of brokenness in this actual historical condition that we find ourselves in, and thus needs continual reconciliation and healing.

At this point I would like to relate one powerful experience right after the reception of the Eucharist which I was privileged to partake in, and which brought home to me in a very concrete way all the dimensions of the Body. The service was held at Perkins Chapel, at the seminary where I currently teach, and it was held in memory of the martyrs for justice in Central America.

As the participating congregation went up in two files to the altar to receive the communion bread ("This is my body, given for you"), a deacon standing beside the communion minister handed each of us a small wooden cross made out of two popsicle sticks pasted one across the other, and with it a small slip of paper to bring back to our pews and keep. On each slip of paper was written a name, a country, and a date. On mine was the small inscription: Victoria de la Roca, Guatemala, Jan. 6, 1982.

After we were all settled back in our pews and after the usual momentary silence, we were invited to stand up one after another and, holding the small wooden cross up high with the right hand, to recite the name of the person written on the slip of paper we received, saying, ". . . Presente!"

It was indeed an event that cut through barriers of time and space as we stood up, one after another, cross uplifted, reciting, "Victoria de la Roca, Presente!" "Jose Bernardo, Presente!" "Estrella Consolacion, Presente!" Each name resounded throughout the congregation, with the proclamation, "Presente!" And still resounding within all of us, with each name, were the words: "This is my body, given for you."

I can only attempt here to describe what went on during those moments, when the Communion of Saints became a living reality before us, in the very here and now, in this very body: "Presente!" All time and all space zeroed in on this "Presente!" And yet, with this was also the tearful realization of the hurt and the sorrow and the injustice and the brokenness that remains in this real world of ours and continues to be a painful reality in the lives of our fellow beings on this Earth community — the wounds of the martyred ones, named and unnamed, remain open in this Body, crying out for healing.

At that moment of "Presente!" the image of all those men and women, young and old, still living or already deceased, that I had met in my many visits to my own country, the Philippines, struggling for their very survival under situations very similar to those the grass-roots communities in Central and Latin American countries are placed in, came to the fore to me in a rather vivid way. They were all right here, with all their struggles and their wounds and their tears, as well as their hopes and their joys and their laughter, "Presente!"

Further, it is not only those persons that I had actually met in some way or another, but every sentient being in this universe that ever lived, continues to live, or will live in the future, that are included, and somehow re-presented, in this "Presente!"

As my eyes are opened to all these dimensions contained in this "Presente," I realize that I carry in this very body all the wounds of the whole Body, wounds that continue to cry for healing. The wounds of the millions of children born into this world malnourished and who are destined to die before they reach the age of five. The wounds of the victims of violence in different forms, whether through armed warfare or other kinds of physical acts of violence wrought by human beings upon one another. The wounds suffered not only by human beings but also by countless other species, and upon Earth itself, with the destruction of our natural life-world because of our human thoughtlessness and irresponsibility. The physical as well as spiritual and all other kinds of wounds brought about by human greed, anger, and ignorance wreaking havoc on individuals, on families, on ethnic communities, on the whole Earth-community itself.

These wounds have been there throughout our history here on Earth, but never has it reached a stage as in this century, wherein we are made so aware of the global extent of our woundedness, already reaching proportions of a woundedness-unto-death.

It is this realization that I carry these wounds in my very body that empowers me to live in a way that I can offer my whole being, this very body, for the healing of the whole Body, which is Earth, in whatever concrete way I may be called to respond in my given situation. The concrete way I am called to respond as one individual member of the whole body would in turn be based on how I realize my connectedness to the whole and how I see my place within the whole Body.

REKINDLING A "BURNOUT"

Those of us who have been exposed to our common wound-edness through our own individual wounds or through those of our fellow beings, and who have come to see the global proportions of such a woundedness, are easily tempted by a sense of powerlessness of it all. "What can I do in a situation that is so immense and so complicated and so deeply embedded in structures that have been there for ages?"

Those of us who may have started with a sense of determination, who have set out aspiring somehow to be an agent of healing through a particular form of social service or volunteer activity, or through more engaged ways in choosing a career and a way of life geared more directly toward the service of others, may at some point in all this, come to what is commonly termed "burnout." This is a state of mind reached by those who, having started out to be at the service of others in our common woundedness, come to be overpowered by it all. In the process, one runs out of steam and is disabled from continuing such a life of service, needing to withdraw for a time (or once and for all, depending on the degree of the "burn").

Zealous individuals who may have started out with a selfless dedication to the tasks involved in the healing of Earth, sacrificing a great deal in terms of personal gain or comfort or worldly success, are especially liable to such burnout after applying themselves to the task for a certain amount of time and realizing that the situation is not getting any better and more and more wounds are continuing to be inflicted. Such a person comes to ask, "What concrete result has all this work of mine led to? What have I made all that sacrifice for?" What may have started out as a sense of solidarity with one's fellow beings or a sense of injustice that needs to be corrected—which led one to aspire to be an agent of healing or a champion of justice—gradually turns into a sense of powerlessness or defeat. One is unable to give any further. There is a sense of total exhaustion from it all, leading one to question the very motivations that led one to begin in the first place.

Behind such self-doubt, one can point out a subtle but very real and deep-seated attachment that needs to be examined and seen in full light: the attachment to the "I" that wants to see results, the clinging to that "good" self of mine that made all these sacrifices for the sake of others and naturally expects something good to come out of all this. It is this "I" that wants to see results, that holds itself up as good in having made all these sacrifices, that loses steam by not seeing the results (or seeing them as inadequate or less than expected), in losing confidence in one's own "goodness."

It is this same "I" that one is now called to let go of, and simply admit its powerlessness, its inefficacy, even its defeat. The final vestige of the delusive self, that part of me which attributes goodness to itself and expects good results from its endeavors, creates a thin film that prevents me from realizing my true self as interconnected with all. I am called to let go of this delusive self and simply recognize, in my powerlessness and defeat, my no-thingness. It is only with this act of fully letting go of the most precious thing we have remaining within ourselves—that sense of our own goodness which is at the root of the attitude that would expect good results from our efforts—that we can be truly free and truly able to hear from the depths of our be-ing, the words, "This is my body, given for you."

But this "letting go" that enables us to be free to see our true self as interconnected with the whole universe is not something we achieve with our own efforts. In those moments when we are overwhelmed with a sense of powerlessness, we are bereft of even the power to let go, either clinging desperately to what we have left or wanting to wallow in this very debilitating and disturbing, and yet also somewhat snug and numb feeling of not being able to offer another hand to anybody or take another step forward. The temptation is to settle into this snug, numb, and cozy feeling and continue in a state almost of suspended animation, in a state of daze, not being able to do anything for months or even years.

Before yielding to such a temptation, it may make all the difference in the world, if we are able to step back and take stock of ourselves, to see what is happening to us. Zen practice can provide an opening to a person in such a situation, as it enjoins us, "Don't *just do something, sit* there."

Such moments, when we are made aware that we are utterly powerless, when the only thing left "to do" is to simply continue "to be" and admit our powerlessness, our no-thingness, can also be the greatest turning point of our lives. Simply "to be," shorn of every trace of power "to do" anything at all, places us at the rock-bottom of what we are, with no trace of self-construct to bank upon or rely on. There is only our pure be-ing, stripped of all its "doing" and its "having." What we are left with, in such a state of total nakedness, is simply, "this very body," breathing in, breathing out. Breathing in, breathing out.

It is here, however, that everything can take a totally revolutionary turn. We are invited to simply be this very body, breathing in, breathing out. In so breathing in and breathing out, as we abandon ourselves totally from moment to moment to the mystery of that Breath, its healing power will take over in us and be the balm for our woundedness, for our brokenness.

In Zen terms, this is settling into a basic state of be-ing that is given expression in shikan taza, or just sitting, as described previously.

Bereft of all do-ing, bereft of all having, simply be-ing, this total denudation of ourselves, a total self-emptying, is what disposes us for the revelation of the full impact of the words, "This is my body, given for you." It is only such a revelation, not our own efforts but the gratuitous and pure work of grace that was right there from the start, in the Breath, waiting for us to be disposed to its reception, that can not only rekindle the burnout we may have gone through, but can also give us renewed energy and a new source of power to give ourselves anew for the healing of this very body, Earth. Just as in the beginning, as the Breath moved over the waters, giving everything in the universe its form and shape and its very be-ing, so the same Breath blows over the dying embers of our wounded body, rekindling the fire in us that will renew the face of Earth.

7.

Coming Home

A Five-Point Recovery

We have now seen various aspects of the Zen way of life, including its basic presuppositions and its fruits, the structure of practice centered on attuning to the Breath, the experience of enlightenment that is the discovery of one's true self, the flowering of that experience in an enhanced awareness of the mystery of ordinary life, and the opening to a vision of interconnectedness with everything realized as this very body. In treating these themes, we have also presented points of resonance with the Gospel message, opening the Christian practitioner to an experiential appropriation of this message and to its concrete embodiment in one's daily life.

We now come back to our central starting point, that is, how all the above relates to healing our woundedness as Earth community. The reader has already seen the connections as we examined particular issues in Zen practice and the way of life flowing from it, but we need to spell out these connections more explicitly, and this is what we will attempt in this last chapter.

In our first chapter we traced the root cause of our woundedness and brokenness in the ego-centered consciousness that takes the helm in our day-to-day life. This mode of awareness marks a distinct line of separation between the "I" as subject and everything else, including the natural world and our fellow human beings, as objects out there, as Other. In regarding the natural world and fellow human beings as Other, there is built up an idealized image of the "I" that is Other to my true self.

Thus, as long as we are confined in this ego-centered consciousness, we continue to live in a way that is in opposition to, and therefore tends to inflict wounds on, nature, our fellow humans, and our own selves. This can be said of our personal life as an individual human being and our corporate life as a member of the various social groupings we find ourselves in and identify with, which we can consider our extended ego. Entrapped as it were in the ego-centered consciousness, we are also overtaken by a sense of cosmic separateness, a sense of displacement and homelessness, an anxiety which can manifest itself in different ways. This is what urges us to implore, with Hui-k'o, the Second Zen Ancestor in China, "Your disciple's mind is not yet at peace. I beg you, please give it peace."

As we have endeavored to lay out in the preceding chapters, the awakening experience in Zen is an event that enables us to break through the ego-centered consciousness and see it as a delusive framework that prevents us from seeing things as they truly are. With such a breakthrough, the sense of cosmic separateness and displacement is overcome as we see our place in the universe, that is, as we are able to see, in a very concrete way, our intimate connectedness with everything in the universe.

Zen awakening, as an experience of realization of our true self, is an experience of coming home. It is an event which, cutting through all those illusory barriers set by the ego-centered consciousness that caused that sense of cosmic separateness, brings with it a deep sense of at-home-ness in the cosmos, at-home-ness with myself, with my fellow humans, with Earth. The awakening also enables us to realize that we have always been there, that we have never been separated or displaced, and yet it is only now that, to paraphrase T. S. Eliot, we know the place for the first time.

In Christian terminology, all the time we thought we were lost in a state of sin, God was there with us. The awakening experience enables us to proclaim with a sense of gratitude that amazing grace wherein we are found. We thought we had been separated from God, but God was never for a single moment separated from us. Like the loving parent in the story of the Prodigal (Lk. 15:11-32), God was always there, waiting, until we were ready to come home. When we finally do, there is endless celebration in the whole household.

The Zen life is no other than that which leads to and, conversely, flows from this deep sense of cosmic at-home-ness, wherein we experience the recovery of everything we thought we had separated ourselves from. The word *recovery* here includes both the retrieval of what we thought had been lost and the return to a state of well-being and wholeness that was our original state in the first place, a state of holiness and blessedness that was there "even before the foundation of the world" (Eph. 1:4).

Coming home includes a five-point recovery: 1) recovery of the *now*, 2) recovery of the *body*, 3) recovery of *nature*, 4) recovery of our *shadow*, and 5) recovery of the *feminine*. Let us look at these five interrelated dimensions that characterize various aspects of our healing, the healing of Earth.

RECOVERY OF THE NOW

As we have seen in the previous chapters, the way of life and spirituality that flowers from Zen's practice can be described simply as a way of *living fully in the here and now*. In short, Zen spirituality paves the way for our recovery of life where it is actually lived, that is, in the reality of each present moment. It thus implies a recovery from a mode of existence that is driven by the pursuit of some ideal of happiness or fulfillment which we project somewhere "out there" in the future, to one that is able to experience and be fully aware of the mystery of the present.

We can illustrate this with an example given by Thich Nhat Hanh in his book *The Miracle of Mindfulness*. Explaining what he means by the key term "mindfulness," the author describes two ways of washing dishes, pointing out that we can wash dishes to get them clean or simply to wash dishes.[1]

Our ego-consciousness tells us, "What else? Isn't that why

we wash dishes, to get them clean?" It seems so obvious that to question it would seem preposterous.

In the same vein, we tend our gardens so beautiful flowers can come up in the spring, so the neighbors can look and say, "Oh, what nice flowers you have in your garden." We take a bus or train, or drive to work, so we can get there and do our job, so we can earn money to support our family, so the children can go to good schools, so they can get good jobs and start their own families, so we can all live happily ever after. And so on with everything else in our life.

Such a mode of life is one we take for granted as normal and as what everybody else does, propelled by a sense of purpose or goal, expressed in the attitude we assume in the very ordinary act of washing dishes. We wash dishes *to get them clean.* We get them clean so we can go on to the next thing we have to do, like going to the living room to watch television, and then get ready for bed so we can get enough energy to get us through the next day's work.

Our lives as human beings seem to be always directed to the pursuit of some purpose or goal which either we have set for ourselves or others have set for us. This can include long-term goals, such as making a great deal of money, becoming famous, achieving success on the corporate ladder, or just working long enough so we can pay off the mortgage and get the kids through college, or short-term goals, such as getting the dishes clean so we can get them out of the way, so we can relax, so we can prepare for the next day's job, so we can keep bread on the table . . . and so on.

We can say that all this is but a consequence of the fact that our existence is conditioned by time, viewed as a linear movement, as a fleeting present which recedes into the past and is rapidly moving toward the future. This time-conditioned nature of our being always prods us to to look toward the future, for something better than our present, for the fulfillment of our hopes, for the attainment of our goals, for the completion of our projects, wherein we imagine lies the key to the happiness we so long for in life. If we exert ourselves now, our efforts will yield their due results in the future. No one questions this fundamental principle of human action. We bank on our hopes for the future as the motivating principle and driving force for living our present.

With such an attitude, we place a value on things based on how they serve our purposes, how they meet our future goals. We place a premium on things that get the job done more efficiently, that is, with less input of time and energy and with better results. This is in order for us to devote that extra time and energy to other things and bring about increased output and productivity.

Also with such an attitude, we tend to treat persons in a similar manner, preferring those who enable us to meet our goals or help us in our purposes. Our human relations then are governed by a principle of selectivity based on how persons and things meet our set goals and purposes, and we tend to treat one another accordingly on this basis.

In living our lives in this way, we notice that everything we do is geared for something other than itself, and we come to realize that nothing is ever done for its own sake, as we keep doing things with a set purpose in mind, beginning with such immediate tasks as getting the dishes clean. Reflecting on the implications of such a mode of life, we find that we go on from day to day always a step away from life itself, as we do everything toward a goal or purpose out there, always ahead of us, and we are never really able to appreciate anything that we do in the present moment for what it is. We are never really able to live life where it is at, that is, in the *here and now.* Everything is always measured by how it meets a future purpose or an imagined ideal, and we miss living the reality of life that is right before us. Even the arrival at a goal, for example, getting the dishes actually clean (where the act of washing them has been performed as the means to arrive at this end) is but a step to the next one, that is, to be able to go to the living room, and then to prepare for bed, in turn to get energy for the next day's work. And what is that next day's work for, but to provide us with the income so that we can go home, wash the dishes . . . and the cycle goes on. So we find ourselves going around in circles, like a dog chasing its tail. We are always chasing after some dream of happiness in the future, and all these things we do in the present are the means toward its attainment.

One can only characterize such a mode of life as a state of separation, a state of alienation from the only life we have to live, as everything is done on account of something other than itself. The fact is, we have come to be deluded into thinking that this is the only way we can live life, bound in time and space as we are, and we continue to look toward the future, perhaps when we retire and do not have to work, to give us relief from this frenzied way of leading life. When we do reach that point, we spend our time looking back, asking ourselves what we might have missed in all this.

In other words, we go on living from day to day, either looking toward that goal in the future, imagining an ideal we have yet to attain, or else looking back at the past, when we may have had things a little better. In this way we never really place ourselves where life is to be lived—right before our very doorstep, in the here and now of each present moment. We go through each day propped up by that imagined ideal of fulfillment in the future, or a glorious past now gone. Thus, we hardly notice how we place ourselves outside of life as we go on day after day—unless the weight of it all gets the better of us and we experience a crisis or near breakdown and are confronted with the question, "What is all this about, anyway?"

Such a mode of life, always driven by something outside of ourself, prodded on from one thing to another, and yet never really able to relish anything, is behind our lack of inner peace, our sense of meaninglessness and frustration, not to mention much of the neurosis and mental imbalance that plagues us and many of our contemporaries.

It is in being confronted with such a question as "What is the point of all this?" and stepping back to reflect on our situation that Zen can open a new door for us. It invites us to a way of life where we take everything from where it is, just as it is, and not for something other than itself, beginning with very simple things in our day-to-day life, like washing dishes.

Zen practice, centered on seated meditation where we simply sit in stillness as we follow every breath, enables us to come back to where the fullness of life is waiting for us: in every here and now. Every breath is lived in its fullness. As one walks, every step is taken without worrying two steps ahead, but just placing one's whole being on *this* step. As one takes tea, one relishes every sip. This mode of awareness, of be-ing fully in the here and now in each given moment, carries on through our daily life. Such is a life that has arrived at a recovery of the *now*.

The Gospel message proclaimed by Jesus is no less an invitation to the recovery of the present moment. "The time is fulfilled. The reign of God is at hand." It is an invitation to open our being and welcome this reign and all that it implies, in the totality of our lives, beginning right here and now (Mk. 1:15). In the very ordinary events and encounters of our life from day to day, we are invited to open our eyes and our whole being to the reality of God's active presence in all this.

Just as Jesus embodied in his whole life the very presence of that reign of God in all that he said and did, those of us who *hear* the message of Jesus are called to embody that reign in our lives, from moment to moment. "Follow me." Right in the present moment.

Jesus extends an invitation to entrust our whole being to the reign of God and not worry about the morrow: "take no thought, saying, 'What shall we eat?' or 'What shall we drink?' or 'How shall we be clothed?' . . . seek first God's reign, and all these things shall be given to you" (Mt. 6:31-33). We are invited to open ourselves to the discovery of that reign of God in every present moment of our lives.

The famous scene of the Last Judgment (Mt. 25:31ff) also gives us a very important pointer in this context of living in full awareness of the *now*. First of all, we may be easily led to take this passage literally as something that will happen in a far-distant future, but a closer look reveals something important for us. In this scene, those who are called to their eternal glory in God's reign are told, "whenever you did this to one of these little ones, you did it to Me." If we listen closely, we can hear the call to be more attentive to the here and now. In other words, the passage is telling us that as we open our being to each and every one we encounter in daily life and respond accordingly with our whole being as the situation calls upon us to, whether it be in offering nourishment or solace to another, simply providing a listening ear, or just saying "hello" —*in that very moment*, right there where the encounter is taking place, God's active presence is discernible. This is the Good News that Jesus proclaims: "in every present moment I myself am knocking at your door, and as you open your being to Me in all these 'little ones,' there I AM, right in your midst."

Another passage from Luke calls our attention in the same direction. "The reign of God is not coming with signs to be observed, nor will they say, 'Lo, here it is, or there.' For behold, the reign of God is in your very midst" (Lk. 17:20-21).

Unfortunately, as the message was handed on to later generations, the community of believers somehow lost this sense of the impinging nature of God's reign in each present moment in our lives, and Christians have tended to look for a fulfillment of that reign in an eschatologically far-distant future. To believe in the Christian Gospel came to mean belief in salvation in an afterlife where everything in this present life will find completion and fulfillment.

The belief in the Second Coming of Jesus the Christ as a future event has tended to cloud his own assurance of his constant presence in our midst, suggested in the words attributed to him throughout the Gospels that "I will be with you always, till the close of the age" (Mt. 28:20).

This, of course, is not to deny the belief in the Second Coming as such, or its significance, in the same way as we cannot and need not deny the phenomenon of time as a linear movement facing the future. What Zen invites us to, however, is a glimpse of that dimension that cuts through time—past, present, and future—that same dimension that was experienced by the author of the letter to the Ephesians, writing in the same breath about the time "even . . . before the foundation of the world," as well as "the fullness of time," wherein all things will be united in Christ, "all things in heaven and things on earth" (Eph. 1:4,10). Zen opens us to a glimpse of that fullness of time wherein past, present, and future come together at zero-point, wherein the whole cosmos is united "in one head, Christ."

The doctrine of the Second Coming of Christ is brought from an attitude of banking on (literally acquiring credits and debits for) a far-distant future, to a stance of constant vigilance in the *now*, as also hinted at by the parable of the wise maidens (Mt. 25:1-13).

Here we can also mention the implications of the dualistic view of Christian teaching as centered on the belief in the after-life—the attitude that makes everything done in the here and now a mere means, a piling up of merits and demerits, credits and debits that will be brought to account in that afterlife. Such a dualistic view is behind the noted criticism that (the Christian) religion offers only a "pie in the sky" that benumbs people's sensitivities to the tasks of the here and now.

In calling our attention back to the here and now, Zen practice thus enables us to recover the original impact of that Good News that the reign of God is already at hand, in our very midst, as we go about the manifold tasks of living from day to day.

We may continue to do exactly the same things from day to day, like washing dishes, tending our garden, going to work, and coming back home. But the way of life that Zen invites us to is one that bears a striking difference from a life that banks only on some expected fulfillment in the future, whether it be in linear continuation of history or in an afterlife.

An important point to note, however, is that we do not deny the phenomenon of our time-conditioned existence, which is what gives meaning to talk about the eschatological dimension. Nor do we reject the concrete possibility of an afterlife. We do not deny the fact that phenomenally and historically speaking we are indeed moving toward the future wherein the complete manifestation of God's reign is promised. As we take this time-conditioned mode of being for what it is, we are invited to center ourselves in the here and now and discover that reign *already at hand*, even as it is *not yet*. We are called to live life there at its source, discovering the fullness therein.[2] Zen is an invitation to a way of life that finds its glory and its fullness in the here and now, opening itself to the encounter with the Holy One right in our very midst.

To put it simply, such is a life wherein we wash dishes simply to wash dishes. Which does not mean to say that they do not get clean. If we are truly able to wash dishes, the natural result is for them to get clean. So we also enjoy the fruits of what we do, as we do them for their own sakes. The difference is that we do things for their own sakes, as we place our whole being upon the here and now, engaging ourselves in our various tasks in life, and not finding ourselves in a state of separation, being driven by the purpose for which we do them. We are able to relish life as it is, taking things just as they are, feeling the touch of the warm water in our hands, our feet on the floor. In all these we open ourselves to the totality of the mystery of life right where we are at every moment, with its ups and its down, its joys, as well as its pains.

To bring in another expression used in the Zen context, we "chop wood, carry water" simply to chop wood and carry water. We are able to meet life where it is, right here, in all its mystery and wonder, as we chop wood and carry water. And lo and behold, as we *do* all this, things fall into place. The wood gets into the hearth, the water gets into the kettle, the fire is lit, and the rice gets cooked. And we partake of the rice, and receive our nourishment, in gratitude.

The recovery of the *now* is the healing of the fissure in our time-bound mode of being caused by our constant pursuit of a projected ideal out there somewhere in the future. This fissure is what impels us to relate to persons and things around us, including everything in the natural world, in a way that treats them as means toward the attainment of our projected goal, and is thus behind the exploitative and utilitarian attitudes we take in these relationships. With the healing of this fissure, freed of such attitudes, we are thus enabled to cherish and treasure our relationships and con-celebrate our being together in the here and now. This recovery of the *now* is thus a vital component in an ecologically sound way of life that enables us to value and celebrate our life on Earth.

RECOVERY OF THE BODY

The recovery of the *now* is connected with the recovery of the body. Our alienation from our own bodies is behind much of our situation of brokenness and woundedness, and its recovery is crucial in our healing.

In Western Christendom, the body has often been regarded as something to be looked down upon, as a source of temptation that deflects the soul from its eternal destiny, as a source of evil that weighs down upon us in our effort to do good. Such a dualistic view that places the body in opposition to the soul has led to an attitude of denigration of anything associated with our bodily existence.

"If it gives pleasure, it must be sinful," goes a saying uttered often in a half-serious manner, but which strikes a chord in the experience of many raised in a traditional Christian atmosphere. Raised as a Roman Catholic in pre-Vatican II times myself, I remember those printed cards placed in the pews in church on Saturday afternoons to help us prepare for confession, enumerating the sins of the body, or better, sins because of the body. Those directives issued by the church regarding the sins one could commit because of one's body, with warnings of eternal damnation due to those sins, did not make it difficult for anyone to feel a tremendous sense of guilt in just having been born as an embodied being, with all the proclivities to sin because of this body.

In such a context, to be a spiritual person meant that one concerned oneself as little as possible with things of the body and did not give in to the gratification of the senses, such as of the palate, of the eyes, of the sense of touch, and others. The ideal was to keep the body in tow and the flesh mortified, so it would not weigh down the spirit in its flight to the divine.

St. Ignatius of Loyola, in his rules for members of the Society of Jesus that he founded, writes on the vow of chastity that each one should strive to be as the angels.[3] Such an ideal of spirituality, which seems to have been quite representative of Christian belief and practice for centuries, easily leads one to lament the fact that one is born as an embodied being, that we are humans with this baggage of flesh that keeps diverting us from that ideal.[4]

This attitude of disdain toward the body that prevailed in Western Christendom for centuries was reinforced by the philosophical view that ushered in the modern era. The Cartesian framework drew a sharp line between mind and body as distinct entities making up our human mode of being. Such a philosophical view lies at the underpinnings of Western culture over the past several hundred years, and is at the root of much of the dis-ease and neurosis found in this culture.

It is only in this century that Western philosophers have presented an understanding of our human mode of existence that tends to overcome such a dualistic view and does better justice to the fact of our embodiment as the starting point in the consideration of our very being.[5]

We can also mention at this point that the attitude of denigrating the body that comes out of a dualistic worldview has now given in to a reactionary tendency that we can characterize as a cult of the body in our contemporary culture. The prevalence and apparent success of commercially motivated body-development programs is a telling indication that many of our contemporaries are eager to reclaim the body with a vengeance.

From a theoretical angle, more recent philosophical and theological developments focus on bodiliness in ways that overcome the dualistic views of past eras.[6] Biblical scholarship also has called attention to the more holistic views of the body in Hebrew Scriptures and New Testament writings as preceding the dualistic tendencies in later developments.

In this connection, the doctrine of the resurrection of the body receives renewed attention as the affirmation of this bodily dimension as central and crucial in the Christian understanding of human existence, to distinguish it from other philosophical or religious worldviews that make the separation of body and spirit an ultimate and unbridgeable one.[7]

Zen practice and the way of life that follows from it opens us to an enhanced appreciation of and sensitivity to the sacredness of our bodily mode of being as we are awakened to the cosmic and earthly dimensions of this bodiliness. This practice and way of life grounds our recovery of the body not merely on the theoretical (philosophical or theological) level but, more significantly, on the level of lived experience, in our concrete, historical, day-to-day life.[8]

The meticulous care given to posture, the focusing of our whole being on the here and now in following our breathing, in taking every step, as well as in the mindfulness of every particular aspect of our day-to-day life, enable us to experience our body in the fullness of its manifold dimensions. *In this very body*, we come into touch with the ultimate dimension of our being. I come to be at home with my own body as my true self, and in being so, I am at home in the universe.

"This very body, the body of the Awakened One (Buddha),"
is a phrase from the Song of Zazen chanted in Zen meditation
halls all over the world, giving expression to this realization of
our body as the locus of the Zen awakening experience.[9]

This realization opens our eyes to the grandeur and mystery
of our bodiliness and enables us to celebrate it as *that which
makes us what we are in our relatedness to everything in the universe*.
This very body *is* the locus of the universe. The universe is given
concrete expression in everything experienced *as* body, from the
moment I wake up in the morning through all the activities and
encounters of the day, even through the hours of sleep at night.
The interconnectedness of everything in the universe is manifested in this very body, a wondrous and unrepeatable configu-
ration of elements of Earth and stardust, given fresh new life
with every Breath.

This sense of interconnectedness with the throb of life of the
universe comes in a most vivid way in the experience of parenting. To gaze at one's own newborn infant, born from a loving
body-to-body union with one's beloved, cannot but fill one with
a tremendous sense of awe, that *in this very body* flows such
unfathomable life and power that can bring about the birth of
this delicate new being, itself bearing this same mysterious life
and power, to continue the process on to the next generation in
its own due time. This unfathomable life and power that flows
through me, in this very body, has flowed through countless
generations before me, and every pulse of mine is connected
with the heartbeat of each and every one of those who have
gone before, just as this newborn life is connected with my own.

Parenting, or gazing at any newborn child, is of course a
common human experience, and the natural sense of awe at the
mystery of life flowing through the universe that accompanies
this experience needs no special effort to conjure. The sensitivity
to this mystery and to the connectedness of all life flowing
through *this very body* can only be enhanced and brought to
further levels and depths. The awakening experience in Zen
opens one to such depths, where one is able to embrace each
and every sentient being in this universe in a very concrete way
as *this very body*. It enables me to say I am the mother of every
child, and I am the child of every mother.

The recovery of the body that is brought about with Zen practice and the Zen way of life thus involves not only the overcoming of the false dichotomy between mind and body that has influenced much of Western culture, and not only the re-appropriation of our bodiliness as the locus of our true self, but likewise the overcoming of the gap between *my* (and only my) body and each and every body. With this overcoming, the pain of every sentient being in the universe is felt as my very own pain, *in this very body*, and naturally draws me to respond, in whatever way I can, toward its healing.

RECOVERY OF NATURE

The ecological crisis that now impinges upon us all and threatens the very survival of the coming generations on this planet is in great part due to the attitude we humans have assumed toward nature. We have considered the natural world as out there, as something to be mastered, controlled, tamed for our human purposes. The critical situation we find ourselves in is rooted in a distorted attitude based on the principle of domination, a cosmological view that only serves to incite our human desire to gain greater and greater control over nature.

The Christian (mis)reading of the Genesis story wherein man and woman are given the mandate to "subdue" and "have dominion" over other creatures (Gen. 1:28) has been noted as a key factor in this distorted worldview.[10] Attempts to explain this story in terms of stewardship or the mandate to care for creation, are being made from within the Jewish and Christian traditions by those who hold on to this story as their own.[11] The significance, not to mention the necessity, of such attempts is not to be gainsaid, but their efficacy still waits to be seen in the actual way members of the Jewish and Christian traditions, both as individuals and as communities, are able to overcome a worldview based on human domination of nature and succeed in presenting and, more importantly, in living out the implications of what many have called for as a new cosmology founded on a vision of harmony and partnership with nature.[12]

Such a new cosmology is a crying need not only for those of

us who continue to look to the Genesis story for an understanding of our place in the universe, but for all of us who have been infected by the so-called modern mentality that separates humans from nature. Our critical situation, brought about by our alienation from the natural world, confronts us as an urgent task that we all need to address together as Earth community.

Multilateral efforts at interreligious dialogue focusing on this urgent task can pave the way toward forging this new cosmology, out of which can come a way of living and relating to nature that would not only be able to forestall impending destruction but would also lead to a regeneration of Earth itself.[13]

A contribution proposed from a theistic perspective is the view of the world, of the entire universe, as God's body.[14] Such a view would indeed open the way for a different attitude toward the natural world on the part of us humans. Rather than treating it as a lifeless machine that runs on predetermined physical laws, we would be able to regard nature as a sacred realm, throbbing with God's own life that nurtures our own.

The contribution that Zen can make toward the recovery of nature, more than in simply providing a theoretical outlook, is first and foremost in the actualization of a way of life that embodies in a concrete way this connectedness with nature. Those who do engage in Zen practice and experience this connectedness with nature as an outflow of their practice are especially called to give expression to their experience and participate in the tasks not only of shaping a new cosmology but of living out its implications.[15]

In this regard, Christians engaged in Zen practice in particular are invited to reread the Genesis story in the light of their Zen experience. There are hermeneutical and theological issues that need to be brought into play, and we will not go into them here, but I will simply indicate one thread that can be pursued in such a rereading of Genesis from a Zen perspective.

Genesis 1:2 provides us with a very suggestive lead, as we read how "the Breath (*ruah*) of God was moving over the waters." This line is very often passed over and not given too much attention, but a Zen practitioner, who is aware of the centrality of Breath in forming one's awareness of reality, will discover a deeply resonating chord in this expression.

It is this primal Breath of God moving over the waters that gives shape and form to everything there is in this universe. In sitting practice, as we focus our attention on the simple process of breathing in and breathing out, the ego-centered consciousness that regards the "I" as in here and the rest of the universe as out there dissolves—is emptied. The terminus of this process is the *emptying* both of the "I" in here and the rest of the universe regarded as out there, to a zero-point where there is *nothing but* this primal Breath, experienced in its full dynamic power. Simply breathing in, breathing out, emptied of ego-centered consciousness, one is able to touch the primal Reality pervading the whole universe.

At this point let me recount the experience of a Catholic sister I was privileged to assist in an eight-day retreat. After several days of silence and breath awareness, she came to an interview with tears of joy and gratitude, reporting how during a walk in the garden she had "breathed the Breath of a flower." This momentary experience had opened to her an entirely different perspective and enabled her to see herself, her place in the universe, and her calling to the religious life in a new light. To make a long story short, she came in touch with the primal Breath in the encounter with the flower in the garden.

"Behold the lilies of the field" (Mt. 6:28), Jesus enjoins us. And if we do not let ourselves be satisfied merely with the theological or ethical lesson to be gleaned from the passage, but really take this as an invitation to *behold* the lilies of the field, there may be something in store for us. In beholding the lilies of the field, we open ourselves to being touched at the core of our being. In so doing, we may find ourselves ushered into a new way of seeing not only the lilies, but everything else in the natural world and the universe as a whole. Sitting practice in Zen, breathing in and breathing out, emptying ourselves and surrendering to the power of the Breath, makes us susceptible to being touched at the core and being transformed by that primal Breath that gives everything its being.

The recovery of nature that the Zen way of life leads to is based on a total surrender to that primal Breath, as we let it be the guiding power in our lives. In doing so, I come to realize in a very concrete way that every flower, every blade of grass, everything in the natural world is given being, as I am given being, in that Breath.

Such a recovery of our connectedness with the natural world does not imply that we humans will simply be passive spectators who are meant only to stand in awe and contemplate the natural processes that go on around us and within us. Our recovery of nature in this context means that in recognizing ourselves as part and parcel of nature itself, we also reclaim the right and the responsibility to participate in the creative activity of the natural world.

Japanese Zen gardens are concrete examples of a way humans can reclaim this connectedness with nature. They are the outcome of a sensitivity to the voices of nature leading to a new creation based on human responses to those voices.[16]

Zen practice and the way of life that issues from this practice can make a vital contribution toward a new cosmology that would ground us in a recovery of nature, as well as a new creation with human participation based on a sensitive listening to the voices of nature. As we have attempted to lay out in different parts of this book, the awakening experience that is at the heart of Zen opens our eyes to our interconnectedness with everything in this universe, to our fundamental at-one-ment not only with other human beings, but likewise with "mountains and rivers and the great wide Earth," as *this very body*.

To see the natural world as one's own body radically changes our attitude to everything in it. The pain of Earth at the violence being wrought upon it ceases to be something out there, but comes to be our very own pain, crying out for redress and healing.

In Zen sitting, breathing in and breathing out, we are disposed to listen to the sounds of Earth from the depths of our being. The lament of the forests turning into barren desert, the plaint of the oceans continually being violated with toxic matter that poisons the life nurtured therein, the cry of the dolphins and the fish, come to be our very own plaint, our own cry, from the depths of our very being.

Our response to these cries heard from the depths of our being will be guided by our concrete situation, from where we

are and in the way we discern our particular role in the healing
of the whole body.

RECOVERY OF OUR SHADOW

A dimension of our existence that depth psychologists have
called to our attention is that of our shadow. This refers to that
"dark" side of our being buried in our unconscious that we
would rather not see, that aspect which we would describe as
negative, destructive, violent, chaotic, evil.[17]

As we look around and within ourselves, we see an interplay
of opposites that make up our concrete existence in this world
bound in time and space: good and evil, beautiful and ugly,
pleasant and unpleasant, creative and destructive, light and
dark, life and death. Faced with these pairs, the "I" or ego-
consciousness, which we posit as the standpoint from which we
view the world, places itself on the side of the good, the beautiful, the pleasant, the creative, on the side of light and life, and
takes an attitude of denying their respective opposites, of disidentifying itself from them.

The ego-centered consciousness which we posit at the center
of our personality (from *persona*, mask, in Latin) thus tends to
idealize itself and identify with the positive side of the pairs of
opposites, in the process denying or dissociating itself with the
negative side. It does so by a mechanism of *suppression* which is
a "deliberate elimination by ego-consciousness of all those characteristics and tendencies in the personality that are out of harmony" with what is valued as positive, or by *repression*, wherein
those negative aspects are simply allowed to fade into the background and become disconnected from consciousness. In doing
so, however, in disidentifying or denying the negative side of the
polar opposites, the ego-centered consciousness creates a rift
right at the core of our being. This paves the way for these
negatives to "lead an active underground life of their own with
disastrous results" for both the individual and the community.[18]
In other words, the suppressed or repressed side of the polar
opposites gathers momentum and comes to the fore with a vengeance, wreaking havoc on the individual as well as on society.

This bipolar nature of our existence as presented by depth psychology is dramatically portrayed in the story of Dr. Jekyll and Mr. Hyde, where the good and evil sides of the same person find themselves acting on different planes unknown to each other, manifesting what is known as a split personality. The unrecognized shadow can continue to remain active and undermine the very status of the good and bright side. We see how such a state of affairs can actually exist in cases where outwardly respected persons come to be revealed as having skeletons hidden in the closets of their personal lives.

Further, we also see how persons deemed to be good and upright citizens or church members, acting as the conscience of the community, can also be the most vindictive, the most judgmental, the most cruel toward those who are perceived as falling short of their moral standards. Such vindictiveness, judgmental stances, and cruelty, depth psychologists would point out, are the outcome of their vigorous efforts to deny the shadow side of their own existence, and this denial projects itself in their attitude toward those they associate with that shadow. "Scapegoating" — laying the blame on some identifiable culprit, whether it be an individual or group or type — is one mechanism arising from the way we humans deal with our shadow side.[19]

On a grander scale, we can see the effects of such a denial of the shadow side of our being as resulting in the hideous episodes of our human history: the innumerable wars fought in the name of some rightful cause; the Crusades, with all their holy fervor at destroying the infidel; the Inquisition, with its religiously and legally sanctioned persecution of those who threatened the belief system of the majority, and so on. In our century, the Holocaust, Hiroshima, Vietnam, the Killing Fields of Cambodia, Gulag, Tiennamen, Sarajevo are salient examples of horrors that we humans have perpetrated in the name of a dazzling ideal, be it "a superior humanity," "a quick way to peace," "democracy," "equality," "order," "ethnic purity," or what have you. Such is the pursuit of an ideal by our ego-centered consciousness, an ideal of the good with that it wishes to identify by suppressing or repressing its opposite or by projecting it on the Other.

Going further, we can also see how our global ecological cri-

sis, an alarming state of affairs that we have wrought upon ourselves, is an outcome of our one-sided worship of the twentieth-
century idol of progress. Assisted by its powerful ministers
named science and technology, progress is identified in an
uncritical way with everything that is good for our happiness,
and yet has been pursued in a manner that has totally failed to
consider its destructive toll on Earth itself.

In short, there opens out a rift at the core of our being as we
give ourselves to the pursuit of an ideal of the good in a way
that is accompanied by the denial of the shadow side of our
existence. Such a rift makes itself manifest in different ways,
coming to haunt us in those abhorrent events and situations in
our individual and communal history. The brokenness and
woundedness in the different dimensions of our being can be
seen as a manifestation of that rift.

The denial of our shadow is but an inevitable outcome of our
mode of living that lets the ego-centered consciousness have its
way. In other words, as long as we live our lives with the I, me,
mine at the center as the controlling factor in our lives, then we
fall into that trap of tending to idealize ourselves and seeing
only the good, the beautiful, the bright side of our being that
the "I" wants to identify with. Consequently, we fail to see the
opposite pole that is also part of us, either by just looking the
other way or by wishing it away or, worse, by suppressing or
repressing it.

This ego-centered consciousness functions not only on the
individual level, but likewise on the corporate level, as we identify ourselves with a larger entity such as a nation-state, a financial corporation, an ethnic group, a neighborhood gang. Such a
corporate ego-centered consciousness takes on the attitude of
"we versus they," wherein "we" arc on the side of justice, truth,
and the good, while "they" are the exact opposite.

We can thus see how a mode of living based on the ego-
centered consciousness that also identifies with corporate egos
on different planes leads to the situation of perpetual conflict
we humans find ourselves in. Whether on the individual or corporate level, the ego-centered consciousness projects its own
shadow on the Other and fights it there, thus contributing to its
own destruction.

The problem of our own death is one important area that comes up in the consideration of our shadow. Death looms in upon us as a constant threat to our very being. In our attempts to assert our being in the face of the nothingness we associate with our impending death, we embark on all kinds of projects to reassert our being in its continued existence.[20] Such projects however, issuing from an attitude of denial of death, can be seen as no more than our desperate efforts to shield our ego from our shadow. They come from what we can term an "edifice complex" in us, where we are driven to build all kinds of make-shift structures that we can lean upon and that provide a convenient shelter for our threatened or wounded ego.

The only way to the healing of that wounded ego is not in our continued efforts to give it shelter from reality, a shield from our shadow, but to let it come face-to-face with this dark dimension of our being. We are called to confront our shadow, face-to-face. For example, looking death in the face is the only way to learn how to live with it and no longer be threatened by it. Paraphrasing the words of the Jesus character in the musical play *Jesus Christ Superstar*, "to conquer death, you only have to die . . . you only have to die."

The recognition of and reconciliation with our shadow is a crucial element in our healing. Recognition and reconciliation involve first being able to *see* that there is a shadow side of our very being and then being able to *accept* it as part of ourselves. Only in the recognition and acceptance of our shadow side can we become whole, integrated, reconciled, and therefore truly and fully ourselves.

This of course does not mean giving in to the power of the negative and destructive side of us, letting it have its sway over us until we become agents of destruction, chaos, and death. It simply means that we break through our mask (*persona*) fabricated by the ego-centered consciousness, the wall concocted by the idealized "I" that identifies only with one side, and allow ourselves to listen to the deeper dimensions of our own being, where the dark side lurks. In those deeper dimensions we will meet not only the good and the bright side that our ego-centered consciousness wants to identify with, but come face-to-face with the evil, the chaotic, the destructive, all that constitutes the darkness and the negative in our historical, communal, and personal existence.

The practice of seated meditation in Zen, where we place ourselves fully in the here and now as we follow our breathing, enables us become more and more transparent to ourselves and thus cut through our ego-centered consciousness to listen to the deeper realms of our being. There, as our practice ripens and becomes more and more transparent to ourselves in both our bright as well as dark side, we may be surprised by a voice — gentle, but clear in a way that leaves no room for doubt — telling us: *That thou art.* It is the hearing of that voice and our full acceptance of all that it implies that can liberate us from the ego-centered consciousness that wants to be identified only with one side, the "good" side of ourselves, and thereby causes the rift in our being.

The hearing of that voice enables us to see in a new light not only the good and the beautiful that our ego-consciousness would have us identify with in a one sided way, but also the evil, the ugly, the chaotic, the destructive, as an inevitable aspect and inseparable part of our very own selves — and enables us to take responsibility for it. Owning our shadow and taking responsibility for it paves the way for us to integrate it with the rest of us, and thus enables us to come to wholeness in our lives.

As we deepen in our Zen practice, we are enabled to reach down to the depths of our true self, touching that point where it is interconnected with everything in the universe. It is at this point where our bright side and dark side meet. It is also the point where we meet our shadow squarely, without having to oppose it or resist it, and simply recognize it, own it, take responsibility for it, and face its consequences with equanimity. This is the point where there is no more fear, for we have reached the realm beyond light and dark, beyond life and death, and find ourselves in the fullness of freedom, having overcome all opposites.[21]

In the Christian creed, the doctrine of Christ's descent into hell, often glossed over or played down in treatment, can be pursued in this context as indicating an encounter and reconciliation with the shadow aspect of our cosmic existence. Zen practice can give us a key toward an experiential appreciation of this doctrine as we are invited to follow Christ in this descent to the netherworld of our being. Such a descent into hell is seen as a condition for the Risen Christ to be a truly integrative power reconciling the principalities and powers, all the warring opposites in the universe, uniting all things, "things in heaven and things on Earth" (Eph. 1:11).

The healing message of the Gospel can also be expressed in the phrase, "The glory of God is the whole human being fully alive."[22] The whole human being fully alive is to be understood as one who has integrated the light and the shadow sides of one's being and has thus come to salvation, to wholeness, and to holiness.

RECOVERY OF THE FEMININE

It has been pointed out by many writers that the civilizations that have prevailed in our human history have operated on the principles of subjugation, exploitation, dominance, and violence. History is witness to the pattern of dominance by humans over nature, by stronger tribes over weaker, by men over women. *Patriarchy* is the term used to describe that mode of being and mode of social relations based on such principles. It is given expression in human actions, as well as in attitudes and institutions that shape our lives.[23]

We can see such a mode of being and mode of social relations as connected to a set of attitudes that are also behind our brokenness and woundedness. This set of attitudes involves a mind-frame that: makes the *now* a mere stepping-stone, a means to a future end; treats the *body* as separate from the mind and as something to be controlled and subjected to the so-called higher faculties; regards *nature* as an object out there to be mastered and tamed, and; avoids the *shadow* side of our existence, denying its presence by suppressing it, repressing it, or by projecting it onto Others.

We have already indicated how Zen can provide the basis to liberate us from these above attitudes and, following the same line, we are also able to see how Zen practice and the Zen way of life offers a way out of that set of attitudes and institutions characterized as patriarchal. This is what we can understand as Zen's contribution toward a recovery of the feminine dimension of our being, referring in different ways to males and females.

The Zen way of life leads to and flows from the experience of awakening to our true self as interconnected with everything in the universe. This awakening is what unleashes the powers of cosmic compassion to be fully at work in us. This experience in turn opens us to a mode of being characterized by *connectedness* and *relationship*, rather than by control; by *cooperation* rather than by competition; by *partnership* rather than by dominance; by *nurturing and caring* rather than by subjugation and exploitation. The actualization of such a mode of being in our personal lives and our social structures and institutions is what we mean by the recovery of the feminine dimension in us.

This characterization of the feminine dimension by the above traits—connectedness and relationship, cooperation and partnership, nurturing and caring—does not mean to imply that *maleness* is identified with the opposite of these traits. Nor do we mean to suggest that only women manifest these traits and that men do not. Here we simply take the view, perhaps often stereotyped and overextended, but useful to a certain extent, that each one of us, of whatever gender, partakes of a masculine and a feminine dimension in our being. Our projected social character is then determined by which of these dimensions takes prominence in our modes of relating with one another. It is in this context that we use the notion "feminine dimension," contrasted with the "masculine," characterized by the traits described above.

In the Buddhist tradition, the feminine dimension is given expression in the figure of Kuan Yin (Japanese, Kannon, short for Kuan Shi Yin, Japanese, Kanzeon, or "Hearer of the Sounds of the World"), the bodhisattva* of cosmic compassion. Kuan Yin is shown as having a thousand arms that can reach in all directions to deliver sentient beings from their sufferings in manifold forms.[24]

The figure of Kuan Yin points to a mode of being whereby, having been emptied of the delusive and divisive ego-centered consciousness and having realized the interconnectedness of all beings in the universe, one hears, and in hearing, *realizes oneness with* the sounds of the world—the cries of children dying of hunger, the plaint of mothers who care for those children; the voices of those silenced and imprisoned and persecuted by the powerful of the world; the cries of the homeless, the refugees, the discriminated; the cries of dolphins grieving at the slaughter of their marine companions by thoughtless humans with so-called efficient fishing methods; the cries of thousands of species of sentient beings going extinct from year to year; the cries of the mountains and forests being denuded.

As one deepens in one's practice and familiarity with the Zen way of life, Kuan Yin is encountered not as something out there, as an object of veneration distinct from oneself, but as the very embodiment of the cosmic compassion that encompasses all of us, that which makes us what we most truly are. The emptying of the ego-centered consciousness in Zen practice, leading to the real-ization of one's true self, enables one to see in full transparency how one is interconnected with all sentient beings, with mountains, rivers, the great wide Earth. This real-ization is the embodiment of Kuan Yin in one's very life. The turning word for the practitioner, for the one who hears the sounds of Earth, is this: *That thou art.*

In the Christian tradition, Mary the Mother of Jesus is looked upon as an embodiment of compassion. The figure of Mary at the foot of the Cross described in the Gospel of John is enshrined in the Latin hymn *Stabat Mater* ("The Mother Stood By"), and has been venerated through the centuries as a figure that people have turned to for help in time of need. Knowing suffering herself, she is able to listen to others with compassion and intercede on their behalf. Her cosmic significance is implied in the Book of Revelations, where she is depicted as "a woman clothed with the sun . . . with child in the pangs of birth, in the anguish of delivery" (Rev. 12:1-6).

The theological significance of Mary is being given new attention, especially in the light of discussions on the feminine dimension of divine compassion. In this context, a particularly suggestive theme is the image of Mary the Mother of God as the model of the church, originally presented by St. Ambrose of Milan (339-397) and taken up in the Second Vatican Council's *Document on the Church.*[25]

In other words, the church, that community gathered together in the hearing and proclamation of the Gospel, is called to a mode of existence modeled on that of Mary the Mother of God, the compassionate one. This means that those of us who profess to be hearers of that Gospel are called to open our whole being to become, as Mary, an embodiment of divine compassion. This is possible not due to our own human efforts, but precisely insofar as we are emptied of our ego-centered consciousness and make ourselves transparent in our being in a way that, like Mary, lets that divine compassion work in us in our day-to-day life.

It is only as we let go of our ego that wants to control and dominate and possess and, like Mary, open our whole being and let ourselves be overpowered by the Breath, letting it take us where it will, that we open ourselves to the work of this cosmic compassion in our lives. Opening ourselves totally to this power of compassion and letting it guide us where it will in the work of healing our wounded Earth is at the same time to open ourselves to a glimpse of the feminine side of the divine at work in the universe.[26]

In conclusion, Zen spirituality ushers in a life characterized by the five-point recovery outlined above. The recovery of the *now* enables us to celebrate life where it is and encounter the mystery of each present moment. The recovery of our *body* enables us to live it as the sacrament of divine presence in the world. The recovery of *nature* is linked also with this awareness of sacramentality and comes to encompass the mountains and rivers, the great wide Earth. We are enabled to hear the cries of Earth, wounded and in pain, as our very own woundedness and pain. The recovery of our *shadow* allows us to face the evil in the world with courage and equanimity and take responsibility for it. And the recovery of the *feminine* is realized as we let go of that part of us that wants to control and dominate and exploit and, instead, allow cosmic compassion to work in our being. Unleashing this cosmic compassion is what effects our own healing and is likewise what empowers us to participate in tasks of healing Earth.

This fivefold recovery takes place with our *coming home*. Ecology (based on the Greek *oikos* = "home"), after all, is no other than coming to know and live in our own home. Zen opens us to a true knowing that enlightens our whole life, in every thought, word, and action. We realize we are at home, as we awaken to our true self interconnected with everything in the cosmos. We have never left home, yet come to know it for the very first time.

Epilogue

Spirituality for a Postmodern Society

For some time now, those of us living in societies influenced by Western European culture (no matter in which hemisphere these may be located) have harbored the idea that with "modernization" we have reached the apex of our historical development. Modern Western society has been thought to be the norm by which all others are to be patterned and toward which these are to be brought.

However, a more comprehensive view of Earth history and human history now gives us a better perspective to see that so-called modern society, with the attitudes and structures it has brought with it, has in fact introduced factors that are behind our present crisis as Earth community.

As many have already pointed out for us,[1] modern society exhibits the following characteristic features, among others: 1) individualism, 2) a dualistic view of reality based on the subject-object, as well as mind-body dichotomy, 3) a mechanized view of nature wherein it is seen as an object for humans to dominate and control, 4) an idealized view of history that is based on the myth of progress, and 5) a masculine-oriented, patriarchal structure of interhuman as well as nature-human relations.[2]

As we examine these features of modernity closely, we will be able see how they are concrete manifestations that stem from a mode of consciousness operative on the individual as well as on the corporate levels of our being. In other words, "modern society" is the historical and corporate manifestation of our ego-centered consciousness.

Now we have come to a point in our history where we are

able to see through the aberrant nature of modern society, with its myths and underlying attitudes toward reality. We are thus made aware of the need for forging alternative directions for our common future, toward a *postmodern* society, as a condition of our very survival as Earth community.

How then are we to envision a viable common future, a postmodern society that will move us toward the healing of a wounded Earth, toward the realization of a communal existence that enables us to celebrate life together, instead of destroying one another and our own selves?

Different scenarios are being presented by those who have seen through the problem posed by modernity, from literary, philosophical, sociological, and other perspectives.[3] Without getting into the details of the arguments from different groups and disciplines that have contributed to the discussion, we take the position that postmodern society, far from being an established fact, remains a mere construct in the minds of many and that we need to make intentional decisions and take concrete steps to bring it about as a viable reality. Let us take the features of modernity outlined above as our take-off point in examining the features of a postmodern society, as a way of mapping alternative directions for shaping our future.

First, a postmodern society will move beyond *individualism*. We will be able to appreciate better the fact that we are not isolated entities but that each one of us comes into being in the context of the web of interrelationships with all of those who share this life with us. This recognition that it is our interrelationships that make us what we are will enable us to overcome the separatist and divisive tendencies that modernist individualism has brought with it. It will not, however, need to negate or make light of the modern advances made in our human consciousness regarding respect for the individual's human rights, personal dignity, and other notions related to these, but will situate these in the context of our interconnectedness and interdependence as Earth community.

Second, postmodernity will move in the direction of overcoming the *dualism* that characterizes our understanding of ourselves and the world and influences the way we live our own bodiliness. This means a move toward a renewed sense of connectedness with the world, understanding the subject-object polarity implicit in our thinking and activity not as a dichotomous mode of being, but as an interactive and mutually participatory relationality. It will usher in a mode of awareness that cuts through the mind-body dichotomy, enabling a reappropriation of our bodily mode of being-in-the-world, in the various dimensions this entails. (See Chapter 6 for an account of elements involved in this mode of awareness.)

Third, postmodern culture will be able to overcome a mechanistic conception of nature. It will see an *organic relationship* in all elements comprising nature, coupled with a recognition of ourselves as an intimate part of nature itself. This way of seeing will free us from the desire to dominate or control nature, but will enable us to participate in the process of its continuing creativity, with the gifts of rationality and foresight that are proper to us as human beings. In seeing nature as a living organism, we will also learn to acknowledge the unpredictable, the mysterious, the *chaotic side of nature*, and not be threatened by this, but accept it and embrace it as part and parcel of the way things are.[4]

Fourth, postmodern society will no longer be held in thrall by the myth of progress. In contrast to modernistic society, which regards itself as the vanguard of history moving on to greater and greater progress due to technological prowess, postmodern society will be able to appreciate as well as appropriate the treasures of antiquity and learn from those societies that were once termed primitive, but which actually present modes of life full of wisdom and insight into our interconnectedness with Earth. It will no longer be tempted to worship the idol of progress for its own sake, always looking toward a better future, but will be able to celebrate life in its now-ness.

Finally, postmodernity will be a *postpatriarchal society* that would accent the feminine dimension of our being and would balance out the undesirable effects of the masculine-dominant character of our lives and our institutions. Such a recovery would move us in the direction of renewed structures of relationships and modes of behavior characterized by cooperation, caring, and nurturing, rather than by competition, exploitation, and destruction.

However, as we indicated above, this postmodern age will not come about in a deterministic way, that is, as an inevitable movement of history. If anything, it will take shape as more and more of us come to the awareness of the criticality of our present condition as Earth community, see the need to go beyond the modernistic mentality and structures of society that have led us to this condition, and make concrete decisions in this regard.

In other words, an *intentional participation* on our part is called for in the birthing of a postmodern world. It will involve a transformation of our consciousness, which will consequently make its effect felt in our self-understanding, in our relationships with one another, and in the structures of society that are the visible manifestations of those relationships. Such a transformation will permeate throughout the various dimensions of our personal and communal lives, in cultural forms, in our religious expressions, as well as in economics, politics, education, in the academy, and so on.

We are all called to play a part in ushering in the postmodern age as we allow ourselves to be transformed in our mode of awareness, learning to overcome the spell of the modernistic outlook within ourselves. It has been repeated often that a new cosmology is needed to replace the old one associated with the modernistic outlook. This new cosmology will go hand in hand with and will also be the basis of a new spirituality for a postmodern world.

Such a spirituality will not provide an escape from the real world, with a misconceived ideal of detachment that sets its hopes on an other-worldly dimension, the kind based on a dualistic conception of reality. Rather, it will be a spirituality which, while leading the individual to a radical detachment from the ego-centric consciousness and its delusive desires, also invites one to a thoroughgoing engagement with our earthly historical tasks, grounded in a vision of connectedness with and compassion for all sentient beings. In other words, it will be a spirituality of engagement that places itself at the service of the healing of Earth community.

In a culturally and religiously pluralistic context, what will carry us through in a postmodern age is no less than a *global spirituality*. By this we mean a way of life in touch with that dynamic, creative power that lies at the depths of our being—the *spiritual*—that is open to receiving nourishment from different religious traditions while being rooted in one or other. At the background of the term *global* here is the view of Earth as a whole, in the way the astronauts in outer space were able to view her and present us with those breathtaking photographs: a view without the marks of national, political, religious, or other kinds of boundaries.[5]

A global spirituality, by its very definition, will not be the monopoly of any one group or religious tradition, but will be the fruit of a creative process involving mutual encounter and dialogue among members of different traditions. It will manifest both a horizontal as well as a vertical movement: the former involves the mutual enrichment arising out of the encounter of religious traditions throughout the surface of the globe, as indicated above; the latter is the downward movement of the human consciousness as it digs in and discovers its roots at the heart of Earth.[6]

Such a spirituality manifests a deepened awareness of our participation in this interconnected web of life we call Earth, and thus shares basic characteristics with what can be called an ecological spirituality. This is a way of life that cherishes and reveres Earth as home (from the Greek, *oikos*, the root of the term *ecology*). Among its features, it gives due recognition to and cares for the *place* where that life is nurtured, is sensitive to and able to celebrate our bodiliness, and is pervaded by a sense of cosmic awe at the interconnectedness of all.[7] It manifests a sensitivity and capacity to listen to the sounds of Earth, including the pains arising out of its woundedness, and is ready to respond in ways that would lead toward healing.

In short, an engaged spirituality that is also global and ecological will take shape based on a common vision of many of us who, though perhaps in different ways, share the pain of Earth's woundedness and feel the urgent need to forge new directions in our modes of awareness and ways of living. Contributions toward this common vision can be made by all of those who are also able to drink from the wellsprings of the rich spiritual traditions handed down to us by our forebears in our life on Earth.[8]

As we have described in this book, at the heart of Zen is the experience of awakening to the reality of our interconnectedness with the whole universe, a reality opened to us as we listen and surrender ourselves to the power of the Breath. This awakening bears fruit in a way of life that impacts the personal, social, and ecological dimensions of our being. Listening to the Breath, the awakened person is able to open her being to listen to the sounds of a wounded Earth, in their concrete manifestations. In so doing, s/he is empowered by the same healing Breath to become an agent toward the healing of those wounds, in the particular ways s/he may be called to respond and carry out concrete tasks, based on her gifts and talents and station in life.

At this point, some may be quick to point out that our description of the possibilities of Zen spirituality given in this book does not exactly tally with the general sociological portrait presented by Zen practitioners and Zen institutions in the Eastern and Western hemispheres today. Those who take a straight look at such a portrait would call our attention to inward-oriented, ahistorical, and quietistic elements associated with Zen communities and institutions,[9] far different from the glowing picture of Zen as a spirituality of engagement presented here. In response, what we have attempted in this book is not so much an account of sociological, cultural or institutional elements of Zen, but rather, a description of the intrinsic structure of Zen spirituality, which can hopefully serve as a reference point for critiquing the sociological portrait of Zen as it exists today. In other words, lived spirituality is the ground for the transformation of outlooks and institutions that shape our mode of being in the world.

This book introduces the basic structure of Zen spirituality, stemming from the Buddhist tradition and yet revealing deep resonances with a life enlightened by the Christian message. It is a spirituality that can enlighten us and empower us in laying the foundations for a veritable and viable postmodern society, as we buckle down and face our enormous tasks of personal and global healing.[10]

Notes

INTRODUCTION

1. See Thomas Berry, *The Dream of the Earth* (San Francisco: Sierra Club Books, 1988), and also, Anne Lonergan and Caroline Richards, eds., *Thomas Berry and the New Cosmology* (Mystic, Conn.: Twenty-Third Publications, 1987).

2. "Right view" is the first of the Noble Eightfold Path presented by the Buddha as a prescription for the healing of the ailing human condition. Our contention here is that the establishment of this "right view" would lead to the unfolding of the other steps called for in this healing process.

3. See also the series of questions in the Introduction to my *Total Liberation: Zen Spirituality and the Social Dimension* (Maryknoll, N.Y.: Orbis Books, 1989), p. xiii.

4. See Raimundo Panikkar, *The Intra-Religious Dialogue* (New York: Paulist Press, 1978). For theoretical implications of such a venture, see the very suggestive essay by Roger Corless, "The Mutual Fulfillment of Buddhism and Christianity in Co-inherent Superconsciousness," in Paul O. Ingram and Frederick Streng, eds., *Buddhist-Christian Dialogue: Mutual Renewal and Transformation* (Honolulu: University of Hawaii Press, 1986), pp. 115-136.

5. See Tosh Arai and Wesley Ariarajah, eds., *Spirituality in Interfaith Dialogue* (Maryknoll, N.Y.: Orbis Books, 1989), for a collection of essays based on actual experiences of intrareligious dialogue by persons from differing cultures. Also, at the Fourth International Conference on Buddhist-Christian Dialogue held in the Summer of 1992 at Boston University, a working group entitled "Practice Across Traditions" met and considered issues involved in such endeavors. This working group has decided to continue to meet periodically and expand the network.

6. See my "No Longer Buddhist nor Christian," in *Buddhist-Christian Studies*, Vol. 10 (1990), pp. 231-237, in celebration of the life of Yamada Koun Roshi, describing his Zen vision as cutting across traditional religious boundaries.

7. Bill Cane, *Circles of Hope: Breathing Life and Spirit in a Wounded World* (Maryknoll, N.Y.: Orbis Books, 1992), for example, provides a very helpful set of suggestions that can be taken in deepening spiritual life for the socially and ecologically engaged.

8. See David Ray Griffin, ed., *Spirituality and Society: Postmodern Visions* (New York: State University of New York Press, 1988), and other volumes of the SUNY Series in Constructive Postmodern Thought, for a presentation of the features of a spirituality that would be in consonance with a postmodern age. See also Ewert Cousins, *Global Spirituality: Toward the Meeting of Mystical Paths* (Madras: Radhakrishnan Institute for Advanced Study in Philosophy, University of Madras, 1985).

1. TOWARD HEALING

1. The twelve-step program of Alcoholics Anonymous, found so effective worldwide and now also adapted to deal with many other kinds of human situations in need of remedy, begins with the recognition and admission of the problem. For an adapted use of the twelve-step program for ecological action, see Albert LaChance, *Greenspirit — Twelve Steps in Ecological Spirituality* (Rockport, Mass.: Element, 1991).

2. There is now a proliferation of books, of varying degrees of convincingness, making us more cognizant of the global ecological situation since Rachel Carson published her *Silent Spring* (Harmondsworth: Penguin Books, 1965) in the sixties. The media have also alerted the public to the general picture, although controversies continue as to the extent of and implications of our current situation.

3. The meeting of the Latin American Conference of Catholic Bishops held in Medellín, Colombia, in 1968, known as the Medellín Conference, following the spirit of Vatican II, which had just finished three years earlier, endorsed the involvement of the Roman Catholic Church in social issues in this continent and adopted the notion of "institutionalized violence" as "a voice crying out to the heavens for justice." For one analysis of the structural nature of world poverty and hunger, see Susan George, *How the Other Half Dies — The Real Reasons for World Hunger* (Harmondsworth: Penguin Books, 1986).

4. This notion of humanity as the consciousness of Earth also derives from Thomas Berry. See his "Twelve Principles for Understanding the Universe and the Role of the Human in the Universe Process," in Lonergan and Richards, eds., *Thomas Berry and the New Cosmology*, pp. 107-108. Number 6 reads: "The human is that being in whom the universe activates, reflects upon, and celebrates itself in conscious awareness."

5. The notion of "the Other" is a theme in recent thought highlighted especially in feminist and deconstructionist writings. See, for example, Simone de Beauvoir's classic *The Second Sex* (New York: Vintage Books, 1974), which develops the Sartrean thesis of "man as Self, woman as Other." See also Rebecca Tong, *Feminist Thought: A Comprehensive Introduction* (Boulder and San Francisco: Westview Press, 1989), especially Chapter 7, "Existentialist Feminism," pp. 195-216. I thank Prof. Millicent Feske, a former colleague at Perkins School of Theology, for her helpful comments in this regard.

6. For an account of the development of ideas on nature, see Max Oelschlaeger, *The Idea of the Wilderness — From Prehistory to the Age of Ecology* (New Haven and London: Yale University Press, 1991), especially Chapter 9, pp. 281-319. (I thank Prof. Roy Hamric of the University of Texas at Arlington for introducing me to this book and its author.)

7. The lives of the founders of the different religious traditions of the world point to their familiarity with such a dimension from direct experience, which they have expressed in their own respective ways, based on differing cultural contexts and conceptual presuppositions. Persons generally called"mystics," cutting across various religions, likewise attest to and live in this dimension that goes beyond the boundaries of our "ego-centered consciousness."

8. Martin Heidegger, *Introduction to Metaphysics* (New York: Anchor Books, 1959). His major work *Sein und Zeit* (*Being and Time*) is an exposition of this fundamental insight.

9. Martin Buber, *I and Thou* (New York: Scribner's, 1958).

10. The work of Roman Catholic theologians Henri de Lubac, Karl Rahner, Edward Schillebeeckx, and others had developed this point since pre-Vatican II times. The recent movement known as Creation Spirituality led by Matthew Fox takes up this insight and develops its implications in connection with contemporary issues, and also calls our attention to the works of Christian mystical writers echoing a similar theme.

11. One could point out the many differences between the Buddhist understanding of *duhkha* and the Christian notion of sin, beginning with a nontheistic versus a theistic presupposition, and so on, but we prescind from these differences in affirming their *resonance* on this point: the human condition is dysfunctional, and is in need of healing.

2. TASTE AND SEE

1. For a standard historical account of Zen from its Indian backgrounds to its developments in China and Japan, see Heinrich Dumou-

lin, *Zen Buddhism: A History*, 2 vols. (New York: Macmillan Co., 1988, 1990), and the more concise and earlier work by the same author entitled *Zen Enlightenment: Origins and Meaning* (New York: Weatherhill, 1979). Recent studies have also come out correcting and "demythologizing" some elements in Ch'an/Zen accounts of its own history, especially regarding the figure of Bodhidharma, and regarding the canonical lists of genealogical succession before the sixth Zen ancestor, Hui-neng. See Whalen Lai and Lewis Lancaster, eds., *Early Ch'an in China and Tibet* (Berkeley: Berkeley Buddhist Studies Series, 1983), and John MacRae, *The Northern School and the Formation of Early Ch'an Buddhism* (Honolulu: University of Hawaii Press, 1986).

2. For English translations with commentaries by twentieth-century Zen masters, see Zenkei Shibayama, *Zen Comments on the Mumonkan* (New York: New American Library, 1974), Koun Yamada, *Gateless Gate* (Los Angeles: Center Publications, 1979, re-issued, San Francisco: North Point Press, 1991), and Robert Aitken, *The Gateless Barrier: Wu Men Kuan (Mu Mon Kan)* (San Francisco: North Point Press, 1991). For quotations used in this book, I have consulted these translations, freely adapting with my own as need arises to emphasize certain nuances.

3. Yamada, *Gateless Gate*, p. 39.

4. See Thomas Cleary, tr., *Transmission of Light (Denkoroku)* (San Francisco: North Point Press, 1990).

5. Yamada, *Gateless Gate*, p. 13.

6. The Diamond Sangha Zen community based in Hawaii, headed by Robert Aitken Roshi, whose authorized successors are now also leading their own Zen groups in mainland United States, derives directly from the Sanbo Kyodan Lineage in Kamakura, Japan. Authorized Zen teachers of the Sanbo Kyodan tradition are also based in different places in Europe, as well as Asia and Australia. See *Buddhist Christian Studies* , Vol. 10 (1990), pp. 231-237, for a provisional listing of teachers in this lineage.

7. Yamada, *Gateless Gate*, p. 147.

8. See Philip Kapleau, *The Three Pillars of Zen* (Boston: Beacon Press, 1965), pp. 204-208. We will come back to this account of the Zen enlightenment experience later on in this book. See Chapter 6 of this book, titled "This is My Body."

9. *Ibid.*, p. 238.

10. *Ibid.*, p. 244.

11. *Ibid.*, p. 250. Kapleau's book is based on the actual practice of the Zen Community of the Sanbo Kyodan, based in Kamakura, Japan. These testimonies derive from practitioners in this lineage. Another

work describing Zen practice based on this lineage is Robert Aitken, *Taking the Path of Zen* (San Francisco: North Point Press, 1982).

12. With the total emptying of the ego, the fullness of joy of being "in Christ" is an experience attested to by Christians. These testimonies, along with many others coming from direct experiences of this sort, with their differences in linguistic and conceptual content, present challenges to a thesis such as the one presented by Stephen Katz in his renowned essay "Language, Epistemology, and Mysticism," in Stephen Katz, ed., *Mysticism and Philosophical Analysis* (New York: Oxford University Press, 1978), pp. 22-74, wherein he categorically states that "there are NO pure (i.e. unmediated) experiences" (p. 26). The nature of these experiences of individuals from widely differing cultural backgrounds that continue to be confirmed in the Zen tradition is an issue that continues to be a matter of ongoing discussion among scholars. For corroboration from another Buddhist (i.e., the Tibetan) tradition of meditation, see Anne C. Klein, "Mental Concentration and the Unconditioned: A Buddhist Case for Unmediated Experience," in Robert E. Buswell and Robert M. Gimello, eds., *Paths to Liberation: The Marga and Its Transformations in Buddhist Thought* (Honolulu: The Kuroda Institute, 1992), pp. 269-308.

13. Of the numerous works now available in English on this intriguing term "emptiness," I have found the work by Frederick J. Streng, *Emptiness: A Study in Religious Meaning* (Nashville: Abingdon Press, 1967), most helpful for conveying its significance to a Western audience. See also Keiji Nishitani, *Religion and Nothingness*, tr. Jan van Bragt (Berkeley and Los Angeles: Univ. of California Press, 1982) for a very lucid philosophical treatment. For accounts of the issues on the ongoing debate on *shunyata*, see John B. Cobb and Christopher Ives, eds., *The Emptying God* (Maryknoll, N.Y.: Orbis Books, 1990); Roger Corless and Paul Knitter, eds., *Buddhist Emptiness and Christian Trinity* (New York: Paulist Press, 1990); Donald Mitchell, *Spirituality and Emptiness* (New York: Paulist Press, 1991).

14. Yamada, *Gateless Gate*, p. 147.

15. Yasutani Hakuun Roshi (1885-1972) also had a significant role in the transplanting of the Zen tradition in the United States. See Rick Fields, *How the Swans Came to the Lake: A Narrative History of Buddhism in America* (Boulder: Shambala, 1981), esp. pp. 231-272.

16. Aitken, *Wu Men Kan*, No. 41. Yamada, *Gateless Gate*, p. 208.

17. See the preface in all the volumes of the series *World Spirituality: An Encyclopaedic History of the Religious Quest* (New York: Crossroad, 1988 and ff.).

18. Kapleau, *Three Pillars of Zen*, pp. 46-49. Rather than "aims" or

"goals," words which still imply a separation of process and result, or "means and ends," I prefer to call these "the fruits of Zen practice."
19. Also see my *Total Liberation*, pp. 1-9.
20. From Dogen's essay entitled "Genjo-koan," which can be translated as "Actualizing Enlightenment." My translation.

3. IN ATTUNEMENT WITH THE BREATH

1. Anthony Mottola, tr., *The Spiritual Exercises of St. Ignatius* (New York: Image Books, 1964), p. 61.
2. *Philokalia,* literally, "Love of the Beautiful and Good." This is a collection of spiritual writings dating from the 4th to the 15th century, dealing with what is known as Hesychasm and the Jesus Prayer. See Kadloubovsky and G. H. Palmer, tr., *Philokalia on Prayer of the Heart* (London: Faber & Faber, 1951), cited in William Johnston, *Christian Zen* (New York: Harper & Row, 1971), p. 80.
3. Mottola, *Spiritual Exercises*, p. 108.
4. See the *Collected Works of St. John of the Cross*, tr. Kieran Kavanaough, OCD, and Otilo Rodriguez, OCD (Washington, D.C.: Institute of Carmelite Studies, 1991), pp. 622-23 for another translation.
5. Fr. Lassalle's pioneering work introducing Christians to Zen practice is noted worldwide. See his *Zen Meditation for Christians* (New York: Open Court, 1974). See also his *Living in the New Consciousness* (Boston: Shambala, 1988).
6. Aitken, *Wu Men Kuan*, No. 37.

4. AWAKENING TO TRUE SELFHOOD

1. See Jon Kabat-Zinn, *Full Catastrophe Living* (New York: Dell Publishing Co., 1990).
2. Aitken, *Wu Men Kuan,* No. 1.
3. For transcriptions of Zen talks or *teisho* on the koan *mu* and how one applies it in practice, see Yasutani Hakuun's commentary excerpted in Kapleau, *Three Pillars*, pp. 63-82; Yamada, *Gateless Gate*, pp. 13-18; Aitken, *The Gateless Barrier*, pp. 7-18.
4. Aitken, *The Gateless Barrier*, pp. 7-9.
5. See Kapleau, *Three Pillars*, pp. 54-57.
6. See the series of negations in the *Heart Sutra*, a short text chanted as part of Zen practice in different languages in Zen halls all over the world. For a scholarly treatment of this sutra, see Donald Lopez, Jr.,

The Heart Sutra Explained (New York: State University of New York Press, 1988).

7. See Chapter 2, n. 13, above.

8. Martin Heidegger, *Introduction to Metaphysics*, p. 86ff.

9. T. S. Eliot, *Collected Poems, 1909-1962* (London: Faber and Faber, Ltd., 1963), p. 222.

10. Dogen Zenji, *Shobogenzo: The Eye and the Treasury of the True Law*, Vol. 1, tr. Kosen Nishiyama and John Stevens (Tokyo: Nakayama Shobbo, 1975), p. 154.

11. Paul Tillich, "You Are Accepted," in *Shaking the Foundations* (New York: Charles Scribner's Sons, 1948), pp. 159-169. I thank Fr. Rafael Davila, M.M., of the Maryknoll Education Center in Houston, Texas, for calling my attention to and sending me a copy of this essay.

5. EMBODYING THE WAY

1. Aitken, *Wu Men Kuan*, No. 7.

2. See Patrick Henry and Donald Swearer, *For the Sake of the World: The Spirit of Buddhist and Christian Monasticism* (Minneapolis, Minn.: Fortress Press, and Collegeville, Minn., the Liturgical Press, 1989), for a comparative account of monasticism in these two major religious traditions.

3. There is a regular newsletter issued by this association, based at the Benedictine Osage Monastery of Peace at Sand Springs, Oklahoma, and the Trappist Abbey of Gethsemani, Kentucky. The new name for the board, as of 1992, is Monastic Interreligious Dialogue (MID).

4. The Zen community headed by Abbot John Daido Loori, based at Zen Mountain Monastery in Mt. Tremper, New York, can be seen as forging a model in this regard. The community at St. Katharina-werk near Zurich, in Switzerland, headed by Sr. Pia Gyger, a Catholic religious who is also a Zen disciple of Yamada Koun Roshi and Robert Aitken Roshi, is another group experimenting with different forms of communal life with an orientation to tasks of reconciliation in the socioecological fields.

5. For an account of this interplay of fullness/emptiness, see my *Total Liberation*, pp. 10-24.

6. Aitken, *Wu Men Kuan*, No. 41. See also my *Total Liberation*, p. 13ff.

7. See Shunryu Suzuki, *Zen Mind, Beginner's Mind* (New York and Tokyo: Weatherhill, 1970), for an account of Zen spirituality as the cultivation of "beginner's mind."

8. See videotape released by Innergrowth Books, Box 520, Chiloquin, OR 97624, featuring Susan Jion Postal's Zen Journey.

9. Chogyam Trungpa, *Cutting Through Spiritual Materialism* (Boulder and London: Shambala, 1973).

10. Kavanaugh and Rodriguez, eds., *Collected Works of St. John of the Cross*, pp. 365-367.

11. The noted scandals related to sexual and financial improprieties of certain meditation teachers in the United States make us all too aware of the pitfalls in this regard on the part of both disciple and teacher.

12. Anchor Books edition, p. 3.

13. Morris Berman, *The Reenchantment of the World* (Ithaca, N.Y.: Cornell University Press, 1981, republished by Bantam Books, 1984).

14. An account of this incident is included in David Friend and the editors of *Life, The Meaning of Life — Reflections in Words and Pictures on Why We Are Here* (Boston: Little, Brown and Co., 1991), p. 187.

6. THIS IS MY BODY

1. See Zenkei Shibayama's commentary in *A Flower Does Not Talk: Zen Essays*, tr. Sumiko Kudo (Rutland, Vt.: Charles Tuttle & Co., 1970), pp. 65-67.

2. See my *Total Liberation*, Chapter 5, pp. 50-69, for a commentary on the Song of Zazen.

3. See the Genjokoan chapter of Dogen's *Shobogenzo*. This is my own translation from the Japanese.

4. Maurice Merleau-Ponty's work, *Phenomenology of Perception* (New York: Humanities Press, 1962) is a noted landmark in this regard, and it was followed by other works from different philosophical and theological traditions, leading to a new awareness of bodiliness that overcomes the dualistic setting of Descartes and the "modern" thought that followed. For a collection of essays outlining major strands on thinking about the body, see Stuart F. Spicker, *The Philosophy of the Body — Rejections of Cartesian Dualism* (Chicago: Quadrangle Books, 1970).

5. See Yuasa Yasuo, *The Body: Toward an Eastern Mind-Body Theory*, ed. T. P. Kasulis (New York: State University of New York Press, 1987), and David Edward Shaner, *The BodyMind Experience in Japanese Buddhism — A Phenomenological Study of Kukai and Dogen* (New York: State University of New York Press, 1985).

6. Pp. 204-208, listed as "A Japanese Executive, K.Y., age 47."

7. The chapter on "Sokushin-Soku Butsu" ("This very mind, the Buddha") of Dogen's *Shobogenzo*. See Nishiyama and Stevens, Vol. 1, p. 17, for a variation.

8. See my *Total Liberation*, Chapter 3, pp. 25-42.

9. In the introductory poem of the *Wu Men Kuan*. See Shibayama, *Zen Comments on the Mumonkan*, p. 10.

10. Thomas Cleary, tr., *The Book of Serenity* (New York: Lindisfarne Press, 1990), Case 91, p. 390.

11. See Ken Wilber, ed., *The Holographic Paradigm and Other Paradoxes: Exploring the Leading Edges of Science* (Boston and London: Shambala, 1982). Karl Pribram's work is published in his *Languages of the Brain* (1971), and developed in synthesis with David Bohm's work in G. Globus, et al., eds., *Consciousness and the Brain* (New York: Plenum, 1976), and R. Shaw and J. Bransford, eds., *Perceiving, Acting, and Knowing* (New York: John Wiley, 1977). David Bohm's work is presented in Ted Bastin, ed., *Quantum Theory and Beyond* (New York: Cambridge University Press, 1971), and in *Foundations of Physics*, Vols. 1(4), 3(2), and 5(1).

12. See Francis Cook, *Hua-Yen Buddhism: The Jewel Net of Indra* (University Park, Penn. and London: Pennsylvania State Univ. Press, 1981).

7. COMING HOME

1. Thich Nhat Hanh, *The Miracle of Mindfulness* (Boston: Beacon Books, 1970), pp. 3-5.

2. The coincidence of the *already* and the *not yet* characterizes the dynamic of the reign of God in our lives. In such a context, a *realized eschatology* such as that manifested in the fourth Gospel is not an oxymoron but is precisely an incidence of this "coincidence of opposites."

3. In contrast to his detailed instructions on the vow of obedience and also on poverty, he brushes off this aspect with a few curt remarks. See his *Rules for the Society of Jesus*.

4. Frank Bottomley, *Attitudes to the Body in Western Christendom* (London: Lepus Books, 1979), provides a good historical account of the development of thought on the body in Christianity.

5. See Stuart F. Spicker, ed., *The Philosophy of the Body — Rejections of Cartesian Dualism* (Chicago: Quadrangle Books, 1970).

6. See, for example, Charles Davis, *Body as Spirit* (London: 1976), for a theological perspective.

7. See F. X. Durwell, *The Resurrection* (London: Sheed and Ward, 1960), for a landmark study in this regard, based on reflection on scriptural sources.

8. See Shaner, *The BodyMind Experience in Japanese Buddhism,* especially the section on Dogen, pp. 129-185.

9. Shibayama, *A Flower Does Not Talk*, pp. 65-67.

10. The noted lecture of Lynn White, Jr., entitled "The Historic Roots of Our Ecologic Crisis," *Science* 155 (1967), pp. 1203-7, referred to "orthodox Christian arrogance toward nature," and pointed to the Genesis story as a basis for the exploitative attitude humans have taken toward the natural world. White's essay has sparked a lively controversy also among Christian circles. See also H. Paul Santmire, *The Travail of Nature – The Ambiguous Ecological Promise of Christian Theology* (Philadelphia: Fortress Press, 1985) for a historical investigation of Christian views toward the natural world. See also William Leiss, *The Domination of Nature* (New York: George Braziller, 1972).

11. The need to go beyond "stewardship," which still rings of an anthropocentric attitude, is beginning to be emphasized among some circles, although "mainline" Christians would still hold on to this as at least a way to overcome the "subjugation and domination" attitude derived from the Genesis story. See Wesley Granberg-Michaelson, *Ecology and Life: Accepting Our Environmental Responsibility* (Waco, Tex.: Word Books, 1988); Anne Rowthorn, *Caring for Creation* (Wilton, Conn: Morehouse Publishing, 1989); Art and Jocele Meyer, *Earthkeepers – Environmental Perspectives on Hunger, Poverty and Injustice* (Scottdale, Penna.: Herald Press, 1991), among others.

12. See Thomas Berry, *Befriending the Earth – A Theology of Reconciliation Between Humans and the Earth*, with Thomas Clarke, S.J. (Mystic, Conn.: Twenty-Third Publications, 1991).

13. Dialogue and cooperation among members of different religious traditions on this shared task is now being seen as of crucial importance. See Sean McDonagh, *To Care for the Earth* (Santa Fe: Bear & Co., 1990); Eugene C. Hargrove, *Religion and the Environmental Crisis* (Athens, Ga., and London: The University of Georgia Press, 1986). The theme of the Fourth International Buddhist-Christian Dialogue Conference sponsored by the Society for Buddhist-Christian Studies, held in Boston, Massachusetts, Summer 1992, was "Buddhism, Christianity, and Global Healing," echoing this timely concern.

14. This perspective is presented by Christian theologians inspired by the Process thought of Alfred North Whitehead, Charles Hartshorne, and others. See also Jay McDaniel's essay entitled "Revisioning God and the Self," in Charles Birch, William Eakin, and Jay McDaniel,

eds., *Liberating Life: Contemporary Approaches to Ecological Theology* (Maryknoll, N.Y.: Orbis Books, 1990), pp. 228-258.

15. Gary Snyder, *The Practice of the Wild* (San Francisco: North Point Press, 1990), is a recent collection that is noteworthy in this regard. Gary Snyder's influence on American thinking on nature is evaluated by Max Oelschlaeger in *The Idea of Wilderness* (New Haven, Conn.: Yale University Press, 1991), Chapter 8, pp. 243-280.

16. For a thought-provoking essay, see Frederick Turner, "Cultivating the American Garden," in *Rebirth of Value: Meditations on Beauty, Ecology, Religion, and Education* (New York: State University of New York Press, 1991), pp. 51-63.

17. See Erich Neumann, *Depth Psychology and a New Ethic* (New York: G.P. Putnam's Sons, 1969), especially Appendix 1, "Reflections on the Shadow," pp. 137-147.

18. *Ibid.*, pp. 34-35.

19. *Ibid.*, pp. 50-58.

20. See Ernst Becker, *The Denial of Death* (San Francisco: Harper & Row, 1973).

21. These reflections on the shadow deserve much more detailed treatment than we can present in summary form in this chapter, in terms of the tremendous significance its understanding can bring regarding our human patterns of behavior. The contribution of Jungian psychology in elucidating this area is of course significant, and the insights of Eastern religious traditions, notably Tibetan Tantric Buddhism, can be further explored in this connection. For example, there are meditative exercises of visualization focusing on evil or demonic figures that are recommended in this tradition, and such exercises are powerful ways of reconciling the practitioner with one's shadow. I am grateful to Dr. Adelheid Herrmann-Pfandt, of the University of Marburg, Germany, for calling my attention to this theme, which she dealt with in an unpublished paper entitled "The Logic of Love: The Peace Policy of the Dalai Lama, Its Origin and Its Consequences." See also Herbert Guenther, *The Tantric View of Life* (Berkeley and London: Shambala, 1972). The contribution of Zen in the understanding of the shadow still needs to be further explored, and I hope to pursue this as a forthcoming task. David Loy, in a still-to-be published essay on "Nonduality and Death," presents suggestive hints along these lines.

22. Attributed to Irenaeus of Lyons (c. 130-c. 200).

23. Feminist and womanist writers, especially in the last two decades, have thrown light on the patriarchal structures in our human attitudes and institutions. See Rosemarie Tong, *Feminist Thought: A Comprehensive Introduction* (Boulder and San Francisco: Westview Press,

1989). Mary Daly, *Beyond God the Father—Toward a Philosophy of Women's Liberation* (Boston: Beacon Press, 1973), has pointed out how Christian male-centered imagery of the divine is inseparably rooted in such structures.

24. See my *Total Liberation*, Chapter 9, "Kuan Yin with a Thousand Hands," pp. 95-103.

25. Walter M. Abbott, S.J., *The Documents of Vatican II* (New York: Guild Press, 1966), p. 92.

26. See Sallie McFague, *Models of God—Theology for an Ecological, Nuclear Age* (Philadelphia: Fortress Press, 1987), especially pp. 97-123, and Leonardo Boff, *The Maternal Face of God: The Feminine and Its Religious Expressions* (San Francisco: Harper & Row, 1987), among others, for explorations on this theme. We can look to Zen for further contributions in this area, as practitioners also conversant with Christian imagery give expression to the manifold dimensions of their Zen experience in terms consonant with the biblical tradition.

EPILOGUE

1. David Ray Griffin, ed., *Spirituality and Society: Postmodern Visions* (New York: State University of New York Press, 1988). See especially the essay by Joe Holland, "A Postmodern Vision of Spirituality and Society," pp. 41-61.

2. This description accentuating the undesirable aspects of modernity does not mean to ignore or belittle its positive contributions, such as the grounding of the notion of human rights, the launching of technological advancements that are useful for nurturing life, the establishment of democratic institutions, among others. We can treasure these achievements of modernity even as we point out and endeavor to overcome the crucial flaws in its underlying attitudes and accompanying structures.

3. See Charlene Spretnak, "Postmodern Directions," in Griffin, ed., *Spirituality and Society*, pp. 33-40.

4. See James Gleick, *Chaos—Making a New Science* (New York: Viking, 1987), Ilya Prigogine and Isabelle Stengers, *Order out of Chaos* (New York: Bantam Books, 1984), and also Alexander Argyros. *A Blessed Rage for Order: Deconstruction, Evolution, and Chaos* (Ann Arbor, Mich.: University of Michigan Press, 1991).

5. See Ewert H. Cousins, *Global Spirituality: Toward the Meeting of Mystical Paths* (Madras: Radhakrishnan Institute For Advanced Study in Philosophy, 1985), and also my essay, "Toward a Global Spirituality:

NOTES   *161*

Buddhist and Christian Contributions," in *Zen Buddhism Today: Annual Report of the Kyoto Zen Symposium*, No. 8, October 1990, pp. 112-123.

6. Cousins, *Global Spirituality*, pp. 137-138.

7. See Jay McDaniel, *Christianity with Roots and Wings* (Maryknoll, N.Y.: Orbis Books, forthcoming), for a detailed account of the features of an ecological spirituality.

8. Charlene Spretnak, *States of Grace: Recovery of Meaning in the Postmodern Age, Reclaiming the Core Teachings and Practices of the Great Wisdom Traditions for the Well-Being of the Earth Community* (San Francisco: Harper, 1991), is one work in this direction.

9. I have described these elements of the sociological portrait of Zen in an article entitled "Christian Love Meets Buddhist Wisdom: Toward a Mystico-Prophetic Spirituality" (forthcoming), originally delivered as a Henry Luce Lecture for the Graduate Theological Union, Berkeley, California, in February 1993. See also my "Christian and Zen Self-Critique," *Buddhist Christian Studies*, Vol. 12 (1992), pp. 175-178. For incisive cultural, socio-historical, and epistemological critiques of Zen, see Bernard Faure's two recent books, *The Rhetoric of Immediacy*, and *Chan Insights and Oversights* (both issued by Princeton, N.J.: Princeton University Press, 1991 and 1993, respectively).

10. Here I acknowledge the inspiration for my explorations in an engaged global spirituality to Dr. Chandra Muzaffar, a noted Muslim intellectual and social critic from Malaysia. In 1987, we were invited to an interreligious conference of social activists held in Bangkok, Thailand, sponsored by the Asian Cultural Forum on Development (ACFOD) then under the directorship of Sulak Sivaraksa. Participants included members of the Buddhist, Hindu, Muslim, Christian, and also Maori (indigenous New Zealand) traditions. In our conversations, Dr. Muzaffar noted how we were all united in a bond of a common *spirituality*, characterized by a stance of solidarity with the suffering and oppressed in our societies and an engagement in the manifold tasks of liberation in our respective contexts. Such a stance shared by the participants cut across our different religious traditions, but was nourished by and given expression within these particular traditions. My contribution in that conference was to present how Zen spirituality grounds such engagement. This book lays out further details of what was outlined in that initial presentation.

Index